I.

The Sailor's Life of Prayer.

" Prayer is the lifting up of a pure mind to God, the pouring out of a contrite heart, with a sure persuasion that God will grant our requests, and give ear to the suit we make unto Him. Do we ask *When* we are to pray? Always, ' without ceasing.' *Where?* In all places. *How?* From the heart; ' lifting up pure and clean hands;' *i.e.,* in faith and love. Our Prayer, feathered with these two things, flieth as an arrow straight to Heaven."— *Archbishop Sandys.*

" Prayer is the first thing wherewith a righteous life beginneth : the last wherewith it doth end."—*Hooker.*

" The best Christian is always the best Soldier; the more of Prayer in my army, the more of victory."— *Gustavus Adolphus.*

The Christian Sailor is a man of Prayer, believing that—

(*a*) Prayer is a duty at all times ;

(*b*) Prayer has the promise of a blessing ;

(*c*) Prayer has been the practice and delight of holy men in every age.

(*a*) PRAYER IS A DUTY AT ALL TIMES.

" My duty towards GOD is to . . . worship Him, to give Him thanks, to call upon Him."—*Church Catechism.*

" Seek ye the LORD while He may be found. Call ye upon Him while He is near."—*Isaiah* lv. 6.

"Call upon Me in the time of trouble."—*Psalm* l. 15.

" After this manner pray ye."—*Matthew* vi. 9.

" Take ye heed, watch and pray."—*Mark* xiii. 33.

" Men ought always to pray, and not to faint."—*Luke* xviii. 1.

" In everything by prayer and supplication with thanksgiving let your requests be made known unto GOD."—*Philippians* iv. 6.

" Pray without ceasing."—1 *Thessalonians* v. 17.

(*b*) PRAYER HAS THE PROMISE OF A BLESSING.

"If thou shalt seek the LORD thy GOD, thou shalt find Him, if thou seek Him with all thy heart and with all thy soul."—*Deuteronomy* iv. 29.

"The LORD is nigh unto all them that call upon Him, yea all such as call upon Him faithfully. He will fulfil the desire of them that fear Him; He also will hear their cry, and will help them."—*Psalm* cxlv. 18, 19.

"The LORD is good unto them that wait for Him, to the soul that seeketh Him."—*Lamentations* iii. 25.

"Thou, when thou prayest, enter into thy closet, and pray to thy Father which is in secret, and thy Father which seeth in secret shall reward thee openly.—*Matthew* vi. 6.

"Ask, and it shall be given you; seek, and ye shall find; knock, and it shall be opened unto you. . . . Your Father which is in heaven will give good things to them that ask Him."—*Matthew* vii. 7, 11.

"Verily, verily, I say unto you, . . .

Whatsoever ye shall ask in My Name, that will I do."—*John* xiv. 13.

" Ask, and ye shall receive, that your joy may be full."—*John* xvi. 24.

" Without faith it is impossible to please GOD ; for he that cometh to Him must believe that He is, and that He is a rewarder of them that diligently seek Him."—*Hebrews* xi. 6.

" This is the confidence that we have in Him, that if we ask anything according to His will, He heareth us." —I *John* v. 14.

"Pray one for another. The effectual fervent prayer of a righteous man availeth much."—*James* v. 16.

(*c*) PRAYER THE PRACTICE AND DELIGHT OF HOLY MEN.

" These all called upon the LORD, and He heard them "—

Abraham : Gen. xviii. 23 ; xx. 17.
Jacob : Gen. xxxii. 9, 28.
Moses : Ex. xxxii. 31, 32 ; xxxiii. 12, 13, &c.
Joshua : Josh. vii. 6-12 ; x. 12.
Samuel : I Sam. xii. 23.

David: 2 Sam. vii. 18-29.

Solomon: 1 Kings viii. 23-53.

Elijah: 1 Kings xvii. 20, 21 ; xviii. 36, 37.

Elisha: 2 Kings vi. 17, 18.

Hezekiah: 2 Kings xix. 15-19.

Jonah: chap. ii.

Nehemiah: chap. i. 4-11 ; ii. 4, 5.

Daniel is an instance of persevering prayer, in the face of opposition and danger. "He kneeled down three times a day, and prayed and gave thanks before his GOD."—chap. vi. 10.

"*Cornelius,* a centurion, a devout man, . . . prayed to GOD always."—*Acts* xi.

The instances recorded in the New Testament of men "continuing instant in prayer" are familiar to all.

JESUS, "our great Example," kneeled down and prayed ; and "continued all night in prayer to GOD."

He prayed for His enemies as well as for His disciples.

The Christian Seaman, too, will recognise the duty of "*kneeling* before his Maker" in prayer, and he will not cease to ask for courage to do so and for grace to persevere in doing so, both at church (when it is possible) and at night and morning.

The Prayers hereafter written down are meant rather to suggest thoughts for prayer than as forms to be always used.

1. They may merely be read over from time to time as suggestive of prayerful thoughts.

2. Or they may be taken as the foundation or keel on which to uprear that ship of daily prayer which must be daily launched to heaven.

3. Or they may be used as forms of prayer, great care being taken to say them from the heart, and thus prevent them from becoming formal.

MORNING PRAYERS

For which there is always time.

On waking lift up the heart instantly to GOD and say:

Glory be to the FATHER, and to the SON, and to the HOLY GHOST; as it was in the beginning, is now, and ever shall be, world without end. *Amen.*

*After turning out, whilst lashing up
and stowing your hammock, say :*

O Holy, Blessed, and Glorious
Trinity, three Persons and one GOD, I
acknowledge Thee to be the LORD.
I thank Thee for my creation, preservation, and all the blessings of this
life. Make me to show forth Thy
praise, not only with my lips but in my
life, by giving up myself to Thy service.

Vouchsafe, O LORD, to keep me this
day without sin, especially the sin of
[*here think of the sins you know you
are most likely to commit*]. Hide Thy
face from my sins, and blot out all
mine iniquities.

Defend me and my [wife, children,
father, mother, brothers, &c.; *remember those for whom you ought to
pray*], and all my shipmates in all
assaults of our enemies ; that we,
trusting in Thy defence, may not fear
the power of any adversaries, through
the might of JESUS CHRIST our Lord.
Amen.

Our FATHER which art in heaven,
hallowed be Thy name. Thy kingdom
come. Thy will be done in earth, as it

is in heaven. Give us this day our daily bread. And forgive us our trespasses as we forgive them that trespass against us. And lead us not into temptation, but deliver us from evil : For Thine is the kingdom, the power, and the glory, for ever and ever. *Amen.*

EVENING PRAYERS

Which may be said after a heavy day's work, or if you have been employed up to the time for turning in.

LORD, have mercy. CHRIST, have mercy. LORD, have mercy.

Our FATHER which art in heaven, hallowed be Thy Name. Thy kingdom come. Thy will be done in earth, as it is in heaven. Give us this day our daily bread. And forgive us our trespasses, as we forgive them that trespass against us. And lead us not into temptation, but deliver us from evil : For Thine is the kingdom, the power, and the glory, for ever and ever. *Amen.*

I acknowledge and confess my manifold sins and wickedness [*men-*

tion any one in particular which comes into your mind]. FATHER, I have sinned against heaven and before Thee. Restore Thou them that are penitent, and grant that I may hereafter live a godly, righteous, and sober life, to the glory of Thy Holy Name. *Amen.*

Into Thy Hands I commend myself [my father, mother, wife, &c. : *remember by name those whom you can remember without trying*], and all my shipmates. Give Thy Holy angels charge over us to keep us in all Thy ways.

In the Name of the FATHER, of the SON, and of the HOLY GHOST, I lay me down in peace. *Amen.*

MORNING PRAYERS IN VERSE.

On waking, or whilst lashing up, thank GOD for His mercies and say :

New every morning is the love,
Our wakening and uprising prove,
Through sleep and darkness safely
    brought,
Restored to life, and power, and
    thought.

Think of your sins and say :

O LORD, turn not Thy face from me,
  Who lie in woful state,
Lamenting all my sinful life
  Before Thy mercy-gate.

Resolve to serve GOD more faithfully
as you say :

Oft in danger, oft in woe,
Onward, Christians, onward go,
Bear the toil, maintain the strife,
Strengthened with the Bread of Life !

Think of your Relations, Friends, and
Shipmates as you say :

LORD, shower upon us from above
The sacred gift of mutual love ;
Each other's wants may we supply,
And reign together in the sky. *Amen.*

EVENING PRAYERS IN VERSE

Before turning in, or before going to
  sleep, thank GOD for His mercies
  and say :

Praise GOD from whom all blessings
    flow,
Praise Him, all creatures here below,

Praise Him above, angelic host,
Praise FATHER, SON, and HOLY
  GHOST.

Confess your sins to GOD as you say :

Grant us, dear LORD, from evil ways
  True absolution and release;
And bless us more than in past days,
  With purity and inward peace.
Through life's long day and death's
  dark night,
O gentle JESUS, be our Light.

*Think of your Friends at Home, and
your Shipmates, and say :*

O GOD, our help in ages past,
Our hope for years to come.
Be Thou our guard while troubles last,
And our eternal home.

Commend yourself to GOD and say:

Hold Thou Thy Cross before my clos-
  ing eyes ;
Shine through the gloom, and point
  me to the skies ;
Heaven's morning breaks, and earth's
  vain shadows flee ;
In life, in death, O LORD, abide with
  me.   *Amen.*

ADDITIONAL PRAYERS TO BE ADDED
AT LEISURE, ACCORDING TO
OPPORTUNITY.

When Outward Bound.

Vouchsafe, we beseech Thee, O GOD, to preserve us Thy servants. Be unto us our Support in setting out, our Comfort on the way, our Shadow in heat, our Shelter in rain and cold, our Rest in weariness, our Refuge in danger, our Harbour in shipwreck; that Thou being our Guide we may reach the station [*or* post] whither we are bound; and at length return unharmed to our own homes; through JESUS CHRIST our Lord. *Amen.*

When Homeward Bound.

O GOD, who didst make a safe way for the Children of Israel through the midst of the sea; and didst lead, by the guiding of a star, the wise men into Thy Presence; grant to us, we beseech Thee, a prosperous journey, and a peaceful time; that by the guidance of Thy holy angel we may safely arrive at our home; and finally may reach the haven of everlasting salvation, through JESUS CHRIST our Lord. *Amen.*

On Commissioning a Ship.

Prevent us, O LORD, in all our doings on board this ship, with Thy most gracious favour, and further us with Thy continual help ; that in all our works begun, continued, and ended in Thee, we—both those who command and those who obey—may glorify Thy Holy Name ; and finally by Thy mercy, obtain everlasting life, through JESUS CHRIST our Lord. *Amen.*

On Joining a Ship.

Almighty and merciful GOD, of whose only gift it cometh that Thy faithful people do unto Thee true and laudable service, grant that I may so faithfully serve Thee in this ship, that I fail not to attain Thy heavenly promises ; through the merits of JESUS CHRIST our Lord. *Amen.*

On Paying Off.

O GOD, the Protector of all that trust in Thee, without whom nothing is strong, nothing is holy, increase

and multiply upon us Thy mercy;
that, Thou being still our Ruler and
Guide, we may so pass through things
temporal that we finally lose not the
things eternal. Grant this, O heavenly
FATHER, for JESUS CHRIST'S sake, our
Lord. *Amen.*

In an Unhappy Ship.

O GOD, give us grace seriously to
lay to heart the great dangers we are
in by our unhappy divisions. Take
away all hatred, all cause for complaint, all misunderstandings, and
whatsoever else may hinder us from
godly union and concord ; that, as there
is but one Body and one Spirit, and one
Hope of our calling, one LORD, one
Faith, one Baptism, one GOD and
Father of us all, so we may henceforth
be all of one heart and of one soul,
united in one holy bond of Truth and
Peace, of Faith and Charity ; and
may with one mind and one mouth
glorify Thee, through JESUS CHRIST
our Lord. *Amen.*

In the Evening.

Visit, we beseech Thee, O LORD, this

ship, and drive far from it all snares of the enemy. Let Thy holy angels dwell within it, and preserve us in peace; and let Thy blessing be upon us evermore; through JESUS CHRIST our Lord. *Amen.*

On a Birthday.

O Almighty FATHER, by whose providence and goodness, I was, as upon this day, safely born into the world. I thank Thee that Thou hast been pleased thus to give me being and life. I mourn that my past years have been spent so little to Thy honour and service; and I resolve, by Thy grace, that henceforth I will endeavour to spend the rest of my life here in Thy fear and love, to the honour of Thy Great Name, through JESUS CHRIST our Lord. *Amen.*

Thanksgivings and Prayers after escape from bodily dangers in Storm or by Accident on board ship.

We praise Thee, O GOD, we acknowledge Thee to be the LORD.

All the earth doth worship thee, the FATHER everlasting.

To thee all Angels cry aloud, the Heavens, and all the Powers therein.

To thee Cherubin and Seraphin continually do cry,

Holy, Holy, Holy, Lord GOD of Sabaoth.

Heaven and earth are full of the Majesty of thy Glory.

The glorious company of the Apostles, praise thee.

The goodly fellowship of the Prophets, praise thee.

The noble army of Martyrs, praise thee.

The holy Church throughout all the world doth acknowledge thee,

The FATHER of an infinite Majesty;

Thine honourable, true, and only SON;

Also the HOLY GHOST, the Comforter.

Thou art the King of Glory O CHRIST.

Thou art the everlasting SON, of the FATHER.

When thou tookest upon thee to deliver man, thou didst not abhor the Virgin's womb.

When thou hadst overcome the sharpness of death, thou didst open the Kingdom of Heaven to all believers.

Thou sittest at the right hand of GOD in the Glory of the FATHER.

We believe that thou shalt come to be our Judge.

We therefore pray thee, help thy servants, whom thou hast redeemed with thy precious blood.

Make them to be numbered with thy Saints in glory everlasting.

O LORD, save thy people, and bless thine heritage.

Govern them and lift them up for ever.

Day by day we magnify thee;

And we worship thy Name ever, world without end.

Vouchsafe, O LORD, to keep us this day without sin.

O LORD, have mercy upon us : have mercy upon us.

O LORD, let thy mercy lighten upon us, as our trust is in thee.

O LORD, in thee have I trusted ; let me never be confounded.

I humbly beseech and implore Thy Majesty, O LORD, that as Thou hast delivered me [or *us*] from the danger of [*here mention it*], so Thou wouldst graciously grant me pardon of my sins, that I may give Thee back the life which Thou hast spared; through JESUS CHRIST our Lord. *Amen.*

O LORD, Thy Providence is above all perils, Thy mercy above all sins. I have seen at once Thy greatness and goodness, O GOD. Thou wast my Anchor, and I am saved: Thou wast my Pilot, and I am preserved; Thine arms were underneath and held me up. Praised for ever be Thou, the GOD of my help! Praised for ever and in every way be the GOD of my salvation. Yea, as long as I live will I praise Thee in this manner. For of Thy mercy, O LORD, it is that I am preserved and live. LORD, let this danger never depart from my mind, that Thy deliverance may never go out of my heart. Make me ever to be mindful of it, and careful of Thee and Thy service all the days of my life; through JESUS CHRIST our Lord. *Amen.*

For one who is in the habit of Swearing and using Bad Language.

O Blessed JESU, who didst turn and look lovingly on Peter when with oaths and curses he thrice denied Thee, mercifully look upon me with the eyes of Thy mercy, that I may weep bitterly for my sin and set a watch on my lips that I no more offend Thee with my tongue ; for Thy merits' sake. *Amen.*

For one who is tempted to the sin of Drunkenness and Uncleanness.

LORD, grant Thy servant grace to withstand the temptations of the world, the flesh, and the devil ; and with pure heart and mind to follow Thee, the only GOD, through JESUS CHRIST our Lord. *Amen.*

On feeling the burden of any sin hanging heavily on you.

LORD, if Thou wilt, Thou canst make me clean ; LORD, only say the word and I shall be cleansed. And Thou, my Saviour CHRIST, Saviour of sinners, of whom I am chief, despise me not, who am bought with Thy Blood, and called by Thy name ;

but look on me with those eyes with which Thou didst look upon Magdalene at the feast and the thief on the cross ; that with the thief I may entreat Thee humbly, Remember me, LORD, in Thy Kingdom, that with the sinful woman I may hear Thee say, " Thy sins be forgiven thee ; " and with her may love much, for many sins—yea, manifold — have been forgiven me. *Amen.*

When some sin that you have committed comes to your mind in which you have not been found out.

Thou, O GOD, seest me ! Against Thee have I sinned and done this evil in Thy sight. I have sinned against heaven and before Thee. Though I go unpunished by man, my conscience accuses me. I am more unworthy than ever to be called Thy son. As Thy grace has led me to know my sin, let it lead me to repentance ; and remembering that the wages of sin is death, may I never again [*here mention the sin*], but henceforth live unto Thee ; through JESUS CHRIST our Lord. *Amen.*

*After you have been found out in some
sin, and are waiting punishment.*

O GOD, give me grace not to com-
plain either with my lips or in my
heart. Bring all my sins to my remembrance, that I may consider how
much I deserve punishment, and how
little I am punished. Though my heart
is hard and my will is stubborn, my
conscience tells me the truth. I have
sinned in such and such [*here mention the sin*]. Help me to go through
my punishment as I ought, taking it
as from Thee, and not from man. Grant
that by it I may be led to see the
exceeding sinfulness of sin, so that
henceforth forsaking sin I may follow
Thee, the only GOD ; through JESUS
CHRIST our Lord. *Amen.*

In Cells or Prison.

Read *Psalm* li. daily, on your knees.

Grant, we beseech Thee, Almighty
GOD, that we who for our evil deeds do
worthily deserve to be punished, by
the comfort of Thy grace may mercifully be relieved ; through JESUS
CHRIST our Lord. *Amen.*

Or this,

O LORD, we beseech Thee, mercifully hear our prayers, and spare all those who confess their sins unto Thee ; that they whose consciences by sin are accused, by Thy merciful pardon may be absolved; through JESUS CHRIST our Lord. *Amen.*

Short Sentences which may be said and thought about when doing Black List on the Quarter-deck in the dinner-hour or at night.

FATHER, I have sinned against heaven, and before Thee ; and am no more worthy to be called Thy son.

Try me, O GOD, and seek the ground of my heart.

Thou, whose nature and property is ever to have mercy and to forgive, forgive me all my sin.

LORD, be merciful to my sin, for it is great.

Make me a clean heart, O GOD, and renew a right spirit within me.

Cast thy burden upon the LORD, and He shall sustain thee.

The wages of sin is death, but the

gift of God is eternal life through JESUS CHRIST our Lord.

O LAMB of GOD, that takest away the sins of the world, have mercy upon me.

When Falsely Accused.

O Blessed JESUS CHRIST, who for my sake wast accused unjustly and unjustly condemned, grant that for Thy sake I may bear this cross, and patiently wait for Thee to remove it. Above all, let me not be tempted to do or say anything which shall justify the accusation. Let no root of bitterness dwell in me either against [*here mention him*], or against those who by his influence are set against me. Make Thou my righteousness as clear as the light, and my dealings ever just as the noonday; who livest and reigneth with the FATHER and the HOLY GHOST, world without end. *Amen.*

Before going on General Leave.

O GOD, who hast been with me in my going out and coming in; my Pilot by sea, and my Guide by land; be with me and bless me now, that ashore as well as on board I may walk in the way of Thy commandments. I know that dangers await me on shore, the companionship of the ungodly; the evil spirit of· drunkenness; the strange woman that flattereth with her tongue; and, above all, the evil inclinations of my own heart. Give me grace to keep a strict and careful watch over myself, and to pray fervently that the tempter may never have any advantage over me. And if through weakness of the flesh I fall into sin, O grant me opportunity to repent at once; and let no earthly pleasure draw me back from seeking Thee when Thou mayest be found; through JESUS CHRIST our Lord. *Amen.*

When Injured by Some One.[1]

Grant, O LORD, that in this injury which I have endured at the hand of [*here mention his name*], I may look

[1] Before using this prayer be very careful to ask your conscience (1) whether the injury was deserved or provoked by your own conduct; (2) whether you forgive "even as GOD for CHRIST's sake hath forgiven you."

stedfastly up to heaven, and, by faith beholding the glory that shall be revealed, may have grace to bless and even to love him; following the example of Thy first martyr, St. Stephen, who prayed for them that persecuted him to Thee, O Blessed JESUS, who standest at the right hand of GOD to succour all those that suffer for Thee, our only Mediator and Advocate. *Amen.*

In Seasons of Bodily or Spiritual Danger.

LORD, be Thou

Within us, to strengthen us;
Without us, to keep us;
Above us, to protect us;
Beneath us, to uphold us;
Before us, to direct us;
Behind us, to keep us from straying;
Around us, to defend us.

Or this,

My times are in Thy hand; Thou shalt answer for me, O LORD, my GOD.

May nothing separate me from the love of GOD which is in CHRIST JESUS our Lord.

For Deliverance from a Besetting Sin.

O GOD, who hast said, " My grace is sufficient for thee," grant me Thy grace now, that I may have strength to resist the sin of [*here mention whatever it is*]. I know I ought to hate and detest all sin, and this one more than all. Fill my heart with Thy love, and let that be my answer to the tempter; that as Thou, O Blessed JESUS, hast died for love of me and to deliver me from the power of this sin, so for love of Thee may I die to sin and daily live more and more unto righteousness; who with the FATHER, and the HOLY GHOST art one GOD, world without end. *Amen.*

On Getting a Badge, or higher Rating, or on being restored to First-class for Conduct.

O GOD, let this earthly blessing be

ever to me a type of my heavenly calling : that as, in spite of my many sins,
Thou hast vouchsafed to me this temporal privilege for my encouragement
in the Service, so forgetting those things
which are behind, I may reach forth
unto those things which are before,
and press toward the mark for the prize
of my high calling in CHRIST JESUS.
Give me grace to count all things but
loss if I may be found in Him—my
SAVIOUR and my GOD. *Amen.*

On Pay Day.

O GOD, may the money which I
have to-day received for my earthly
service, teach me the priceless value of
that life eternal, which Thou hast freely
given me in CHRIST JESUS ; and grant
that by a right use of it I may learn to
live soberly and righteously in this present world, as one who will have one
day to give account to Thee for all the
blessings, earthly and heavenly, which
Thou hast entrusted to his care ;
through the same JESUS CHRIST our
Lord. *Amen.*

To be used by Officers.

O GOD, who hast said, "The powers that be are ordained of GOD," grant that I may realise the nature of the stewardship to which I have been appointed. Help me so to govern myself, my body, my heart, and my mind, that I may fitly govern those whom Thou hast entrusted to my command, in Thee, and for Thee ; through JESUS CHRIST our Lord. *Amen.*

By Petty and Non-commissioned Officers.

Almighty GOD, by whose grace one petty officer [*or* non-commissioned officer] in the gospel is known to us for his faith, and another for his prayers and good works, grant unto me the same grace that I may ever remember whose authority I exercise towards those who are placed under me ; and by faithfulness, patience, and courage, so perform my duty to them and my commanding officer, that I may be accepted of Thee. For the merits of JESUS CHRIST, who though He was the

Captain of my salvation took upon Himself the form of a servant for my sake. *Amen.*

By Masters-at-Arms and Ship's Corporals.

Make me, O GOD, ever to have before me the example of Thy servant, John Baptist, who was not afraid constantly to speak the truth and boldly to rebuke vice. Give me purity of heart, and true courage that in the discharge of my duties I may have no fear but the fear of offending Thee, and no desire but the desire of pleasing Thee ; through JESUS CHRIST our Lord. *Amen.*

To be used by a Boy.

O LORD JESUS CHRIST, who whilst upon earth didst shew obedience to all who were set in authority over Thee, and when a Boy didst learn willingly and answer wisely, grant me Thy wisdom, teach me Thy patience, and fill me with Thy love. Help me to refuse the evil and to choose the good that, whether in my mess, on deck or ashore, I may ever act as in Thy sight, and suffer every evil rather than offend Thee by thought, word, or deed. Make me honest and smart in my work, willing and cheerful in my mess, true and faithful to my home. Bring me through this ship as through life, a humble and sincere Christian, remembering my confirmation vows, and using Thy manifold means of grace until I reach Thy perfect manhood; through whose merits I say—*Amen.*

For grace to Resist the Advice of those who would Lead us to do Wrong.

LORD, I know that this advice is evil. My own bad heart inclines to it, but Thy voice within me bids me follow Thee. Grant me strength to resist instantly and resolutely. I am weak, but Thou art strong. Help me now to gain one little victory for Thee, and lead me on from strength to strength till I am not ashamed to stand before Thee, in and through the merits of JESUS CHRIST our Lord. *Amen.*

By Servants.

LORD, give me grace to discharge the duties of my service with a pure heart and a diligent hand. Be my support under difficulties, and my strength in temptations. Make me patient and teachable, not only with the good and gentle, but also with the froward. Increase my faith that I may do my work as in Thy sight, and strive to remember in all my dealing with others that I am Thy servant; through JESUS CHRIST our Lord. *Amen.*

On being Tempted to be Wild and Reckless.

Try to fix your eyes in faith on our SAVIOUR, and consider how amidst enemies without and temptations within He laboured for your salvation, and never ceased till through hunger and thirst, through blows and nakedness, through suffering and death, He had bought you with His precious Blood. Say with what heart you can :

O my SAVIOUR, surely it is better

for me to abstain from sin, and to suffer any self-denial, rather than to offend aganst this great love of Thine for me. Warm my cold heart with Thy love. Restrain it, bend it, break it altogether, that it may own no love but Thine, and desire nothing but to be renewed by Thee every moment of my life. *Amen.*

For a Sentry going on Guard.

O GOD, guide my thoughts and keep my heart during my guard. As I walk my post give me strength to do my duty thoroughly and manfully, and to resist all temptation to ease or slothfulness. Fill me with an ever-increasing sense of Thy presence and always support me with the blessed example and merits of Thy SON, JESUS CHRIST our Lord. *Amen.*

TEXTS AND SHORT PRAYERS WHICH MAY BE USED AT THE TIMES AND ON THE OCCASIONS SUGGESTED.

When doing any work on deck or below, which does not require the attention of the mind, as, for example, coaling ship, hauling on ropes, "up

ashes," *cleaning wood and bright*
work, at the lee wheel, scrubbing
decks, and the like.

Whatsoever thy hand findeth to do,
do it with thy might.

Whatsoever ye do, do it heartily as
to the LORD, and not unto men.

Thou GOD seest me.

Not with eye service, as men plea-
sers ; but as the servant of CHRIST
may I do this from the heart, because
it is the will of GOD.

When Tempted to Drunkenness.

Whether I eat or drink, may I do
all to the glory of GOD.

No drunkard shall inherit the kingdom of GOD.

Do not for the sake of drink destroy
the work of GOD.

When Tempted to Swear.

Above all things, swear not, lest ye
fall into condemnation.

Help me, O LORD, to set a watch
before my mouth, and to keep the door
of my lips. *Amen.*

When Tempted to be Angry without cause.

Vengeance is mine, I will repay, saith the LORD.

A soft answer turneth away wrath.

Give me, O GOD, the patience and gentleness of JESUS CHRIST.

When Tempted to join the Company of Bad Men.

My son, if sinners entice thee, consent thou not.

Have no fellowship with the unfruitful works of darkness.

My GOD, give me courage now to say, No.

I am weak, but Thou art strong.

When Tempted to join the Company of Bad Women.

Come unto Me all that travail and are heavy laden, and I will refresh you.

LORD, help me, or I perish.

What is a man profited if he shall gain the whole world and lose his own soul.

How can I do this great wickedness, and sin against GOD.

When Tempted to Skulk during Work.

Could ye not watch with Me one hour?

Be not slothful in business, but serving the LORD.

Well done, thou good and faithful servant; thou hast been faithful over a few things.

When Ridiculed on account of Religion.

The LORD is on my side, I will not fear what man doeth unto me.

LORD, make me to endure to the end, that I lose not the crown of life.

LORD, give me the courage of the three children, who, for love of Thee entered the burning fiery furnace.

II.

𝕿𝖍𝖊 𝕾𝖆𝖎𝖑𝖔𝖗'𝖘 𝕷𝖎𝖋𝖊 𝖔𝖋 𝕮𝖍𝖗𝖎𝖘𝖙𝖎𝖆𝖓 𝕯𝖚𝖙𝖞. [1]

HOLY BAPTISM.

HAVE you been baptized? or christened? which means the same thing. It may seem a strange question to ask. If, however, you cannot answer "yes" to it, do not let another hour pass without making up your mind that you will be baptized as soon as you can. Our Captain—the great Captain of our salvation—ordered every one to be baptized, "In the name of the FATHER, and of the SON, and of the HOLY GHOST" (*Matthew* xxviii. 19). The Apostles obeyed this command as long as they were alive; and in one day baptized as many as 3,000 people in one city (*Acts* ii. 41). Before the Apostles died, they ordained others to

[1] *For much in this and the following chapter, the compiler is indebted to two Mission Tracts published by Longhurst.*

carry on their work. You will have no difficulty in finding some one who is commissioned to baptize you. Not only is it right that you should be baptized, because JESUS CHRIST has commanded it ; but further you have no title to the name of Christian unless you are baptized. He said, "Except a man be born of water and of the Spirit, he cannot enter into the kingdom of God" (*John* iii. 5). Ever since these words were uttered they have been understood of Christian Baptism. As soon as St. Paul found out what a mistake he had been making in fighting against CHRIST and His disciples, he went and was immediately baptized, and his sins were then and there washed away. This is a great mystery. The Chaplain or any well instructed Christian will explain it more fully to you ; but no one can explain it so that you will be able to understand it thoroughly. Shew your love to GOD by obeying His command. Make sure that you are one of GOD'S children by being first washed and renewed by the HOLY GHOST (*Titus* iii. 5).

CONFIRMATION.

You have heard of this word before. In the training ship many of the boys were confirmed, perhaps you were one of them; if you were, these few words will bring back to you some of the thoughts which filled your mind when the Bishop laid his hands upon your head. If you have not been confirmed, what I am going to say will, I hope, shew you that it is your duty to be confirmed without delay. To be confirmed means to be made strong. Who is there that does not need to be made strong in his Christian profession?

In Confirmation we are made strong by the power of the HOLY GHOST, given in the laying on of hands. The HOLY GHOST made us Christians in Baptism. In Confirmation He strengthens us that we may become perfect Christians. He is the giver of life, and this life He gave us in our baptism. In Confirmation He comes to strengthen the life He gave. And as we can be baptized but once, so we can only receive Confirmation once in our lives. Those who are going to be confirmed must prepare themselves carefully in two ways : (1) They must be truly sorry for past sin; (2) they must have faith in GOD'S promises. Then when you have received the gifts of the HOLY GHOST in Confirmation, you must not let them lie idle (1 *Thessalonians* v. 19), else you will lose the power of using them, just as a man who gives up walking, in time loses the power of using his legs. There is much more to be learnt about Confirmation, but enough has been said here to set you thinking about it seriously. Your Chaplain will instruct you ; the Prayer Book will instruct you (see the Order of Confirmation) ; above all, read the following passages in the Bible, and the HOLY GHOST Himself will instruct you.

Look at the following texts in con-nection with Confirmation :—

Acts i. 3, viii. 17, xix. 6, viii. 16, 17 ; Hebrews vi. 1, 2 ; 1 Corinthians xii. 4 ; Galatians v. 16, 22 ; Ephesians iii. 16 ; 1 Corinthians xiii. 8, xii. 31 ; xiii. 1, 2 ; Luke ix. 1, 2 ; John vi. 70,

71, xii. 6 ; Daniel xi. 1 ; 1 Corinthians
xii. 13 ; Titus iii. 4 ; Psalm lxviii. 28 ;
Romans viii. 11, 12, 13 ; John iii. 5,
xiv. 26 ; Colossians i. 11.

*If you are doubtful whether to be Con-
firmed or not say this short prayer :*

O loving LORD, giver of grace,
bring me back into Thy path from
which I have strayed ; teach me what
is good for my soul, and lead me to
seek Thy Holy Spirit in Confirmation,
through JESUS CHRIST our Lord.
Amen.

*When you are preparing for Confir-
mation say daily these prayers :*

O Almighty GOD, who, of Thy
great mercy, didst make me Thy child
in Holy Baptism, help me to prepare
to receive the gifts of the HOLY GHOST
in Confirmation. Give me true and
deep repentance for the sins of my
past life (especially . . . .) ; give me a
firm faith in Thee ; strengthen me,
that I may have grace and courage
to fight manfully, as a true soldier of
JESUS CHRIST, against the temptations

of the world, the flesh, and the devil. Help me to continue Thine for ever, and to suffer anything rather than forsake Thee. This I beg for JESUS CHRIST'S sake. *Amen.*

Almighty GOD, I beseech Thee to bless Thy servants who are preparing for Confirmation, especially . . . Turn them unto Thyself with their whole heart, and increase in them the gift that Thou hast given them in Holy Baptism ; through JESUS CHRIST our Lord. *Amen.*

There is a special privilege in store for you after Confirmation ; namely, admission to the Holy Communion. Persons may receive Holy Communion without having been confirmed, if for some cause or other they cannot be confirmed when ready and desirous to be so. This is often the case with those who live on board ship. After you are confirmed you should receive Holy Communion on the first opportunity. For our Lord has said, "Except ye eat the flesh of the Son of Man, and drink His blood, ye have no life in you" (*John* vi. 53). So that we cannot be good Christians without Holy Communion, even after Baptism and Confirmation ; for we should lose the benefit of them ; just as a man cannot keep life and strength in him without meat and drink. The Prayer Book by appointing a fresh Collect, Epistle, and Gospel at Holy Communion for every Sunday and Holy Day in the year, shews us in what light the Church would have us consider this Sacrament. Further, whilst it orders every one to receive Holy Communion " three times a year of which Easter to be one " it adds the words "at least," showing that it does not mean that we are to receive three times a year only. We may be sure that JESUS CHRIST meant us to receive Him often when He said, " This do in remembrance of Me," and " Drink ye all of it."

SELF-EXAMINATION.

" Let a man examine himself and so let him eat of that Bread and drink of that Cup."

How will the Seaman, who wishes to live godly in CHRIST JESUS, find the time and the place to carry out this command of St. Paul? But, first, what *is* the command? That before receiving Holy Communion a man ought to examine himself.

The Prayer Book explains this by telling us that people should ask themselves four questions : (1) Whether they repent them truly of their former sins, stedfastly purposing to lead a new life ; (2) whether they have a lively faith in GOD'S mercy through CHRIST ; (3) with a thankful remembrance of His Death ; and (4) whether they are in charity with all men.

How, then, shall we find out whether or not we have Repentance, Faith, Thankfulness, and Charity? By placing ourselves alongside the rule of GOD'S Commandments. This seems an easy thing to say, but the Sailor knows that for him it is no easy thing to do.

First, *where* shall he carry out this examination of conscience? There are times when the mess is quiet, especially in the afternoon watch at sea. In a ship where the hands make and

4

mend clothes on Thursday, it will be quite easy to find a place where with all around him he may yet be alone with GOD. If he can find no better place, let him not be afraid to examine himself as he walks up and down the forecastle smoking his pipe. A great deal can be done for GOD when a man is smoking, and if he finds that in a noisy, crowded ship he can do his business best in that way then GOD will accept it. But it is not good for a man to stow himself away. This attracts needless attention and prevents him from obeying any sudden call of duty.

And now *when* shall a man examine himself? Some of the best times have already been noticed. If he is inclined to be sleepy at the mast-head or on the look-out on deck, it will help him to keep awake if he begin to examine his conscience. But it is not good to choose such times except as a remedy for some evil, such as sleepiness or bad thoughts, for the Christian seaman ought above all others to be a *smart* Seaman. The Chaplain if asked would gladly allow the use of his cabin to any

man for the purpose of self-examination, and let him choose his own time.
There are some very valuable intervals
of time which occur in every ship,
which are generally wasted, and which
a Seaman who *wants* to get time for
thought will have little difficulty in
using. These are after the decks are
cleared up and the bugle has sounded
off "cooks," before dinner and supper,
when ropes have been coiled down, or
the brass rags have been returned and
the watch on deck wait only the pipe
to go below. The hours for meals—
the first watch at sea (after the singing
is over)—the middle watch at sea
(directly after the watch has been mus-
tered, or better still, if there is "op-
tional," after that has been served out)
—the times between cleaning and
quarters, or between shifting into
night clothing and quarters, all these
will suggest five or six precious minutes
which a man will use who is on the
look out for them.

A few words are added on the best
way of conducting the examination.

It is a good thing for a man to ex-

amine himself, not only before coming
to Holy Communion, but every day.
If he does so, and thus gets into the
habit of doing it, it is astonishing how
much easier he will find it than if he
examines himself only at rare intervals.
He ought never to begin without lifting
up his heart to GOD the HOLY SPIRIT
to beg for a blessing on His work.
Then let him adopt one of the following
courses.

(1) Think carefully over the events
of the day, beginning from the time
when he turned out of his hammock in
the morning watch, asking himself
some such questions as these : Was my
first thought about GOD? Did I say
my prayers? Did I resolve to avoid
some particular sin during the day?
Did I swear or use any bad language?
How did I employ my thoughts between lashing up and breakfast?
Talking or listening when scrubbing
decks? Or when cleaning the mess
or lower decks? When cleaning myself? At quarters for cleaning guns?
At divisions? At Prayers? Did I
pray at all then? Watch on deck?

Or watch below? On Sentry? And so on. The principal events of the day will be fresh in his memory. His conscience may generally be safely trusted to tell him when he has done wrong. In this manner he will at last arrive at the time when he is making the examination, if he is doing it just before turning in. Or he may divide the examination into two parts—devoting five minutes to it in the dinner hour, and five minutes again in the evening. This will relieve the memory. Then let him gather up in a moment the sins he remembers by name, and make a note of them. He will probably have time then to say the short prayer for forgiveness on page 14; or, he may cry to GOD from his heart using his own words, and begging GOD to give him strength to break with these sins.

(2) Or if he has time, especially on a Sunday or Thursday afternoon, let him examine himself by the rule of GOD'S commandments with the help of the following questions,—first of all saying this prayer :

Almighty GOD, who knowest my inmost thoughts and canst not therefore be deceived, assist me in this my examination that I may see how I have offended Thee in thought, word, and deed.   By repenting of my sins let me obtain Thy pardon and peace; through JESUS CHRIST.

First Commandment.

Do I try to love and serve GOD with *all* my heart?   Am I in the habit of trusting in myself or others instead of in GOD?

Have I neglected my duty to GOD, such as prayers, reading the Bible, Holy Communion, for fear of being laughed at by my messmates or shipmates?

Do I aim at doing all my daily duties as in GOD'S sight?

Do I willingly make companions of those who mock at religion?

Am I proud of my talents, religion, repentance, or any good I have done?

Second Commandment.

Do I attend Divine Worship on board or on shore as often as I can?

Am I in the habit of being irreverent or inattentive in Church? Can I call to mind any occasion of the sort?

Have I the courage to kneel at worship? And do I try to remember GOD'S presence?

Do I read the Bible as GOD'S voice speaking to me?

Third Commandment.

Have I used the name of GOD, or of JESUS CHRIST lightly?

Have I used profane language? Cursing? Or swearing?

Do I do anything to check bad language in others when I have the opportunity?

Have I made jokes on Scripture subjects?

Have I spoken evil of the Chaplain?

Have I spoken against the Church?

Fourth Commandment.

Do I do my best to keep Sunday and the festivals of the Church as the Bible and Prayer Book teach me, by reading the Bible, special prayer, and receiving Holy Communion?

By Officers.

Have I done my best to promote religion amongst the men?

Have I assisted the Chaplain in his duties when I have had reason to know that my assistance would be valued?

Do I set a reverent example at Public Worship?

If I am in authority, have I stopped all unnecessary work on Sunday, and enabled the men to spend it as a day of rest from ordinary work?

Have I caused the great Holy Days of the Church—Christmas Day, Easter Day, The Epiphany, Ash-Wednesday, Good Friday, Ascension Day, to be recognised as well as I could?

Fifth Commandment.

Is there anything in my habit of life which causes my parents sorrow? or would cause them sorrow if they knew it?

Do I render them the support which I ought?

Have I disobeyed the commands of

my superiors either openly or behind their backs?

Have I been civil and kind to my messmates?

Have I honoured the Queen and all who bear rule in her name, in my language? in my actions by performing them honestly and heartily?

Sixth Commandment.

Have I intentionally done any bodily harm to any one, except in the service of my country?

Have I given way to anger in thought, word, or action?

Have I been hasty? passionate? or sulky?

Have I refused to be friendly with any one?

Have I tried to be friendly with any one who has cut me? or whom I have offended?

Have I hurt any one's soul by bad example? or persuasion?

Have I made mischief or stirred up quarrels?

Do I expose my life to danger by

evil living? by drunkenness? in any other way?

Have I tried to lead to repentance those whom I know to be living in sin? Do I ever pray for them?

Seventh Commandment.

Have I been guilty of any immoral conduct?

Have I looked at filthy objects, pictures, books or papers? or witnessed immoral sights, indecent plays, immodest dances?

Have I allowed myself to be idle?

Have I used impure or obscene language? told obscene stories, or stories with double meanings? sung or listened to obscene songs?

Have I been amused by others doing so?

Have I indulged in indecent recollections? [1]

---

[1] Our subtle enemy will under the pretence of Self-examination lure us on to dwelling on past sins of thought, word, or deed, until we shall desire to commit them afresh. It should be noted that with this view the Self-examination is ordinarily confined to the sins of the past 24 hours (p. 52). Old sins, especially of impurity long since mourned over,

Have I been guilty of intemperance in eating? or in drinking?

Eighth Commandment.

Have I taken anything belonging to another?

Have I done my best to find the owner of anything I have found?

Have I injured things belonging to others?

Have I wastefully expended Government stores?

Have I got into debt knowing I could not repay?

Have I smuggled anything on which I ought to pay duty?

Have I given alms according to my ability?

Have I robbed others of any advantage by evil report?

Have I fudged accounts or returns?

Ninth Commandment.

Have I told a lie, even in fun?

confessed to GOD, and we may hope forgiven, should not be again dwelt on. It is a temptation to be carefully avoided.

Have I told more or less than the truth?

Have I told a lie to screen others?

Have I acted a lie?

Have I spoken contemptuously of superiors or messmates?

Am I fond of talking of others' faults?

Have I attributed wrong motives to others or judged others hastily?

Have I broken my word or told a secret confided to me?

Have I abused or ridiculed others maliciously?

Tenth Commandment.

Have I wished for things or talents which GOD has not given me?

Have I been jealous of another's promotion?

Have I been dissatisfied with my lot in life?

Have I been discontented with the duty allotted to me?

Have I wished for the praise of men?

Have I desired greater ease or enjoyment without earning it?

Do I gamble?

What are my habits with regard to betting ?

(3) Another plan is for him to think of those sins which most easily beset him. Then let him take these one by one, and see if he has committed them that day, and how? and when? and where? and with whom? These thoughts will bring other sins to his recollection which he will note.

One word in conclusion. It is not necessary, or even desirable to write these sins down on paper. "The heart knoweth its own bitterness," and there are very plain reasons why it would be unwise to make any written records of one's short comings. It will suffice if, like wise mariners, we examine the frail vessel in which we have to navigate life's ocean, and see wherein she is defective through the assaults of the enemy ; and the inexperience or treachery of those who have the charge of her.

III.

The Sailor's Life of Sacrifice.

HOLY COMMUNION.

IF there be one command of JESUS CHRIST more plain spoken than another, it is " This do in remembrance of Me." If there is one duty which the seaman neglects more habitually than another, it is that of receiving the Holy Communion of CHRIST'S Body and Blood.

Ignorance, want of Courage, and Prejudice, are the three principal causes which keep away the god-fearing seamen from the table of the LORD in the present day. The first is gradually being removed. It is one object of this little book to remove the ignorance which prevails upon the nature of the Holy Communion. But who can supply courage to the timid soul? He only who gave Timothy courage to make "a good profession before many witnesses." Let not the Sailor, however, over-rate the difficulties which he thinks will beset him when he comes to Holy Communion. Of inward difficulties and struggles against his sins we will not now speak. Outwardly he fears the ridicule of his messmates and topmates. Against this there is no remedy but prayer for a brave and single heart. The thought of all that Jesus suffered to obtain redemption for man, will often stir us up to a little courage, and help us to suffer a little for His Name's sake. Again, he fears misrepresentation. He will be told he goes " aft " to be " seen of men "—to get into the officers' good books—to obtain a rate, or some worldly advantage. If these things are false let him not be unfaithful to his Lord and Master, because he is afraid to shew his shipmates they are false, by a steady " continuance in well doing." The hypocrite may well be kept from coming to Holy Communion a second time by the persecution and chaff—which is deserved in

his case ; but not the humble minded
man who wishes truly to turn over a
new leaf, and to begin a life of duty to
his Redeemer.   Lastly, there is much
Prejudice against receiving Holy Communion on board ship—owing chiefly
to the manner and rarity of its celebration.   Let the Seaman reflect that the
Chaplain will make the best arrangements that he can, and then let him
simply obey his Saviour's command ;
whether it be in the Captain's fore-
cabin, or on deck before all hands.
He must not say he will wait until he
goes on leave, or gets his discharge ;
such an answer is an insult to Almighty
GOD.   And what if he should never
live to receive Holy Communion
ashore ?   Let him think of this as he
reads *John* vi. 53.

SHORT INSTRUCTION ON HOLY COMMUNION.

Holy Communion has two objects—
the first is the forgiveness of your
sins ; the second, the strengthening of
your soul by the Body and Blood of
CHRIST.   I will try to explain these.

I.—In heaven JESUS CHRIST is always offering or showing Himself to the FATHER that our sins may be forgiven. CHRIST pleads with the FATHER, that is, reminds His FATHER of His death upon the cross. When you come to the Holy Communion you will do on earth what CHRIST is doing in Heaven. You will remind GOD that JESUS CHRIST died for you. You will ask Him for CHRIST'S sake to forgive your sins. This is what St. Paul says, " As often as ye eat this bread, and drink this cup, ye do shew the LORD'S death till He come" (1 *Corinthians* xi. 26).

II.—By Holy Communion your soul is strengthened. At the Last Supper JESUS CHRIST took bread and blessed it, and said, THIS IS MY BODY. He then took the cup of wine. He blessed it, and said, THIS IS MY BLOOD. You will find the account of this in Matthew xxvi. 26–29 ; Mark xiv. 22–25 ; Luke xxii. 14–20 ; and 1 Corinthians xi. 23–29. CHRIST'S own words must be true. In the Holy Communion JESUS CHRIST comes to feed our souls

spiritually with His Flesh and Blood.
You must come in repentance and
faith, and believe that then He will
give Himself to you. In this special
way your soul will be made truly strong
to fight against temptation.

The week before you receive the
Holy Communion should be made a
week of preparation. Never let a
night pass without one thought about
the great blessing which you are going
to receive. But do not let either the
prayers in preparation, or the devotions
during the service, distress you. They
are meant to help, not to hinder.
Oftentimes only a small part of them
can be used. They will not be too
long for those who are in harbour ships
where there is a regular routine, and
plenty of spare time which can be
reckoned upon. Use, therefore, just
as much of these devotions as you find
helpful.

THURSDAY.

On this day you should begin your
self-examination—thinking over all
you have done wrong since your last

Communion. If you want assistance you will find the Chaplain always ready to help you in this difficult task. He will advise you how to overcome your bad habits, and, if you wish for it, help you to come to Holy Communion with a quiet conscience, as God promises through him to give peace to your soul. That the Chaplain should be your friend is the advice of the Church, as well as of the Admiralty instructions ; as the following words will shew :

" And because it is requisite that no one should come to the Holy Communion but with a full trust in GOD'S Mercy, and with a quiet conscience," —if you feel your conscience troubled with any weighty matter, in which you require counsel and advice, your Church directs you to " go to the Minister of GOD'S Word, and open your grief, that you may receive the benefit of absolution, with ghostly counsel and advice." [1]

[1] First exhortation to the Holy Communion in Book of Common Prayer.

If he has already advised you, you will know what to do. · When you have tried to remember your sins, think how much GOD loves you and wishes you to be saved. Ask Him to make you truly sorry for your sins, and to help you to lead a new and better life, in the following prayer :

O LORD JESUS, Saviour of the world, who camest to save sinners, and saidst, Come unto Me all that travail and are heavy laden and I will refresh you, behold I, a sinner, come to Thee for forgiveness. I have wandered from Thee like a lost sheep. But thou art the Good Shepherd who didst lay down Thy life for Thy sheep. Bring me back again to Thy fold, and let me not any more go astray lest I perish everlastingly. I come to Thee, wash my many sins away. LORD, if Thou wilt, Thou canst make me clean. Make me clean by Thy precious Body and Blood, and help me to serve and love Thee with my whole heart, and bring me at last to Thy heavenly Kingdom. *Amen.*

FRIDAY.

All the blessings you receive come from the death of CHRIST. You ought therefore on Friday to think about His death and sufferings, and to try to be thankful for them. Remember that He laid aside His glory as GOD, and became a weak and suffering Man for *your* sake. He was hungry, thirsty, sorrowful, despised, and at last crucified. He now humbles Himself so much that He gives Himself to you in the Blessed Sacrament of His Body and Blood. Think how very forgetful you have been of His great goodness. You should read a passage of Holy Scripture and think about it. The Gospel for the day will often be very suitable ; or else you may read part of the history of the Passion. You will find this in Matthew xxvi. and xxvii. ; Mark xiv. and xv. ; Luke xxii. and xxiii. ; John xviii. and xix. The following passages refer to Holy Communion : Matthew xv. 32-39, xxii. 1-14 ; Mark v. 24-34 ; Luke xiv. 12-24, xv. 11-32, xix. 1-10 ; John ii.

i-11, vi. 1-14, vi. 43-63, x. 1-18, xiii. 1-17. Then say the following :—

Almighty and everlasting GOD, who, of Thy tender love toward mankind, hast sent Thy SON, our Saviour, JESUS CHRIST, to take upon Him our flesh, and to suffer death upon the cross, that all mankind should follow the example of His great humility ; mercifully grant, that we may both follow the example of His patience, and also be made partakers of His resurrection, through the same JESUS CHRIST our Lord. *Amen.*

Grant, O LORD, that I may receive the sacrament of the Body and Blood of Thy SON JESUS CHRIST, our Lord, with a thankful remembrance of His death for my salvation. Hear me for JESUS CHRIST'S sake. *Amen.*

SATURDAY.

When you come to Holy Communion you remind GOD of His promise to give whatever you ask for in His SON'S Name. You offer and present the sacrifice of the Body and Blood of CHRIST for the forgiveness of your own sins, and those of the whole world. Your prayers will be especially heard at this time; for you will be pleading the death of CHRIST in obedience to His commandment. You should therefore try to remember what you want to pray for, either for yourself or for others.

Think—(1) What sins of your own, or of your friends, need forgiveness. (2) What grace or blessings you or they need for soul or body.

It is well each time you come to Holy Communion to recall *one or two* sins which you are in the habit of committing, and *one or two* blessings which you especially need, and to pray very earnestly to GOD for pardon and help. It is better to pray earnestly for a few things than coldly for many.

During the Day therefore, and if possible in the Evening, try to find time to say :

O Holy FATHER, who didst so love the world as to give Thine Only Begotten SON, that whosoever believeth in Him should not perish, but have everlasting Life,

Have mercy upon me, a sinner.

O Blessed JESU, who didst taste death for all men, and hast promised to accept all such as come to Thee; cast me not away from Thee, but

Have mercy upon me, a sinner.

O Blessed SPIRIT, whose sacred fires melt the hardest heart, who leadest sinners to repentance, and art the Comforter of the sad and wounded soul? do Thou guide me, keep me, comfort me, and

Have mercy upon me, a sinner.

O ever Blessed TRINITY, in whose image we are created, restore in me that heavenly likeness, and

Have mercy upon me, a sinner.

Prayer to Jesus for Pardon, and Grace to persevere in Holiness.

O LORD JESUS CHRIST, Saviour of the world, who mercifully invitest sinners to Thy Cross, that they may be cleansed from their sin; I come to Thee, whom my sins have pierced, humbly believing that Thou art able and most willing to receive me, and wash away the guilt and stains of my past sinful life, and make me clean.

Look upon me, O LORD, as Thou didst on the penitent thief, and have mercy on me ; and as Thou, out of very love, didst pray for Thy murderers, do Thou intercede for me, that Thy blessed Passion, and all-sufficient Sacrifice, may atone for my offences.

O my SAVIOUR, let me never more crucify Thee by my sins, but by virtue and merit of Thy Cross give me true sorrow for my past sin, strength to overcome temptation, and grace to persevere in all good works unto the end.

O Thou, who hast said, " If I be lifted up, I will draw all men unto Me," draw me, LORD, to Thyself. Let nothing henceforth separate me from Thee.

Receive me, O Thou loving Shepherd of souls, receive me Thy poor wandering sheep. Crucify in me the flesh, with its lusts ; root out all evil tempters, and renew a right spirit within me.

Kindle in me an earnest desire to devote myself wholly to Thee, who hast "so loved me, and given Thyself for me." *Amen.*

To be said daily, as opportunity offers, during the Week of Preparation.

O LORD JESUS CHRIST, who hast promised that they who come to Thee shall never hunger, and they who come to Thee shall never thirst : feed me, I pray Thee, with the Bread of Life ; give me to drink of the Water of Life.

Thou, Good Physician, be pleased to heal the diseases of my soul, strengthen and refresh me.

Visit, O LORD, and cleanse my conscience, and prepare my heart to receive Thee worthily in this Blessed Sacrament. *Amen.*

O most merciful FATHER, do THOU receive me, and grant that, though unworthy, I may of Thy Mercy and Grace receive the Bread that cometh down from Heaven, and the Blood that is drink indeed ; for the sake of our

LORD and SAVIOUR JESUS CHRIST; to whom with Thee and the Holy GHOST be all glory, now and ever. *Amen.*

SUNDAY.

Before the Service.

The preparation is now over. Nothing remains now but for the faithful soul to watch for the coming of her Lord. Yet experience has shewn that a Seaman who has prepared himself, and is fully purposed to receive the Holy Communion, has at the last moment held back, owing to some unexpected trouble which has come to him. He has had a job of work to do which he did not reckon upon, has got wet through and had but little time to shift; has had some words with a messmate, or has had some fault found with him at divisions. He is tempted to feel then that his work of preparation is all undone, and that he is no longer fit to receive the Blessed Sacrament. But let him not yield to this temptation. Let him remember that his work of preparation was done hon-

estly and with a good heart, and that
it was a preparation for communion
with JESUS CHRIST.   This breeze will
pass away as quickly as it came, and
nothing will calm the troubled waters
of his mind so much as the sweet presence of Him who, said to the waves of
Galilee, " Peace, be still."   Before this
Saviour—mighty to save to the utter-
most—he will see plainly that the early
morning's trouble was nothing but a
device of Satan, to try and cheat him
altogether of the heavenly gift.

If there be an early celebration of the
Holy Communion, by all means let it
be chosen in preference to a later one,
if possible.   We then begin the day
and the week in the best way, and
moreover we are fresher.   Should a
Seaman find that an early service is
more helpful to him than a later one,
let him not hesitate to speak to the
Chaplain about it.   He would generally
be able to make arrangements.   It
is quite a common thing in some ships,
to have a celebration in the breakfast hour, beginning when the bugle
sounds off " cooks."

A WORD TO READ AFTER DIVISIONS.

The Christian Sailor will call to mind the nature and dignity of the duty he is to perform : that he has to join in the highest act of Christian Worship by celebrating the memorial of CHRIST'S Death, according to His command, who Himself instituted it, "for the continual remembrance of His atoning Sacrifice." " He is the very Paschal Lamb, which was offered for us upon the Cross : " but He is also our High Priest, ever living to plead in Heaven that one Sacrifice, on behalf of each Member of His Church, to the end of time. And what our High Priest doth in Heaven, He commands His Ministers to do on earth. He " did institute, and in His Holy Gospel commands us to *continue a perpetual memory,*" *i.e., Memorial,* " of His Precious Death until His coming again." The oblation of Bread and Wine, which the priest consecrates in the same words which our SAVIOUR used, and of which all partake, is thus a true and lively representation of the

one Sacrifice which was offered on the
Cross, a continual pleading and appli-
cation of the Atonement.   The Jewish
sacrifices, wherein the blood of animals
was poured forth, and the flesh con-
sumed upon the Altar, were appointed
by GOD, to plead before Him the
atoning Sacrifice which was yet to
come.   In themselves they had no
efficacy "to take away sin."   In the
Christian Oblation, "which we are
commanded to continue," He is
pleased that His Church should com-
memorate, and plead the merit of
His Death, "until His coming again."
This commemoration is the Worship
of the Christian Church, as foretold
by the Prophet Malachi : "My Name
shall be great among the Gentiles ;
and in every place incense shall be
offered Me and a pure offering."
For, says the Apostle, "as often as
ye eat this Bread, and drink this Cup,
ye do shew forth the LORD'S Death
till He come."   Thus, the LORD'S
Supper is rightly called a *Commemo-
rative* Sacrifice.

It is also a *Eucharistic* Sacrifice,

ın which the whole Church unites to offer praise and thanksgiving to the LORD. Herein, also "we offer to GOD our souls and bodies, to be a reasonable, holy, and lively Sacrifice unto Him."

AT THE CELEBRATION OF THE HOLY COMMUNION,

Whilst others are going away say humbly :

" How amiable are Thy Tabernacles, O LORD of Hosts.

" My soul hath a desire and longing to enter into the Courts of the LORD :

" My heart and my flesh rejoice in the Living GOD.

" O send out Thy Light, and Thy Truth, that they may lead me :

" And bring me unto Thy Holy Hill, and to Thy dwelling ;

" That I may go unto the Altar of GOD, even unto the GOD of my joy and gladness."

O LORD JESUS CHRIST, who hast bidden all that are weary and heavy-laden to come unto Thee, and dost this day offer Thyself to refresh them ;

at Thy call I come, unworthy as I am of the least of Thy mercies. Sick, I come to the Physician of Life ; unclean, to the Fountain of Mercy ; poor and needy, to the Lord of heaven and earth ; humbly beseeching Thee of Thy goodness to heal my sickness, to wash away my defilements, to enrich my poverty, to clothe my nakedness, that so I may receive Thee with true faith and humility, with love and thankfulness ; and that this Holy Communion may be unto me the remission of sin, and the preservation of soul and body unto eternal life. *Amen.*

Follow carefully the Service in your Prayer Book ; referring to this Book only during the long pause, when others are communicating. At such times you can turn back to the prayers between pages 68 and 75, and offer such portions of them as time permits ; or say the Hymn, " Rock of Ages," or others for Holy Communion. As much as possible, be ever " looking unto JESUS, the Author and the Finisher," the " High Priest over the Church of GOD", the memorial of hose death you are celebrating.

Before going up to the Lord's Table,
say :

Like as the hart desireth the water
brooks, so longeth my soul after Thee,
O GOD.

My soul is athirst for GOD, yea, even
for the living GOD.

LORD, I am not worthy that Thou
shouldst come under the roof of my
soul.

O Lamb of GOD, that takest away
the sins of the world,

Grant me Thy peace.

O Lamb of GOD, that takest away
the sins of the world,

Have mercy upon me.

Before Communicating in either
kind, say :

" What reward shall I give unto the
LORD, for all the benefits that He hath
done unto me ?

I will receive the Bread of Heaven :

I will receive the Cup of Salvation :

I will call upon the Name of the
LORD."

6

After Reception.

Blessed be Thou, O LORD, who hast vouchsafed to feed me with Thy most precious Body and Blood.

Abide with me, O LORD JESU, now and evermore. *Amen.*

Returning to your place, say :

I adore Thee, O my GOD, and glorify Thy Holy Name.

Thou art my REDEMEER, my KING, my GOD ;

Whom have I in heaven but Thee? and there is none upon earth, that I desire in comparison with Thee.

Praised be the LORD, daily ; even the GOD who helpeth us and poureth His benefits upon us.

May Thy love, O LORD, entirely possess my soul, that I may evermore give myself to Thy Service !

If time permit, repeat *Psalm* xxiii. or *Psalm* cxxxviii. Join heartily in the Hymn which concludes the Service, " Glory be to GOD on high," and which formed a part of the earliest Christian Worship.

After the Blessing, say:

O GOD, the Father of our LORD JESUS CHRIST, I thank Thee that Thou hast permitted me to partake of this Heavenly Feast.

O purify my heart ; and do Thou keep me, guide me, strengthen me, subdue me : preserve me from the enemy, and in Thy mercy be pleased to dwell in me evermore.

O make me to be numbered with Thy Saints in glory everlasting ; through our LORD JESUS CHRIST. *Amen.*

Blessed JESUS, the Good Shepherd, who didst lay down Thy life for the sheep, and dost feed them with Thine own Body and Blood, I thank Thee for Thy Mercy, who hast permitted me to join in celebrating this memorial of Thy death, and to partake of this Heavenly Food. LORD, suffer me no more to wander from Thee ; but guide my steps in the way of Thy commandments. Give me strength to fulfil my duties faithfully. Make me a good soldier of Thy Cross ; and grant that, stedfastly cleaving to Thee by love and obedience, I may hereafter behold Thy face in glory. *Amen.*

And now take all possible care not to lose the blessing you have received, by entering into temptation. Go about your ordinary work in your ordinary way, and let no one notice anything in your manner, unless it be that your work is done better and more cheerfully. But with the time that you have to yourself be very careful. If, for example, you are going ashore, see with whom you go, and where you go. Remember that the great enemy of souls is now more anxious than ever to take from you the seed sown. Say as little as is necessary in your mess, and if anything is said to you about what you have been doing, either make no reply, or give that "soft answer" which "turneth away wrath." Occupy some of your spare time in the afternoon and evening in reading the following prayers and meditations.

O LORD JESU, the Strength of our life, who givest us richly all things to enjoy : I heartily thank Thee, that Thou hast been pleased to feed me, Thy unworthy servant, with the Heavenly Food of Thy precious Body and Blood ; and humbly I beseech Thee to grant that all we who have knelt at Thine Altar this day may evermore dwell in Thee, and Thou in us. Pardon the wandering thoughts, the weakness of faith, and whatever else Thou hast seen amiss in our Service of Thanksgiving ; and grant that being refreshed by this Heavenly Feast, we may go forth strengthened for our Christian warfare ; that so, having fought the good fight, we may win the Crown, and enter into the joy of our LORD. *Amen.*

" Now unto Him that loved us, and washed us from our sins in His own Blood, and hath made us kings and priests unto GOD, His Father : to Him be glory and dominion for ever and ever." *Amen.—Revelation* i. 5, 6.

" Worthy is the Lamb that was slain, to receive power, and riches, and wisdom, and strength, and honour, and glory, and blessing." *Amen.— Revelation* v. 12.

O LORD JESU CHRIST, who saidst unto Thine Apostles, " Peace I leave with you, My peace I give unto you ; " regard not our sins, but the faith of Thy Church ; and grant Her that peace and unity which is agreeable to Thy will ; who livest with the FATHER and HOLY SPIRIT, one GOD for ever-more.

O Blessed LORD, who in the wonderful Sacrament of Thy love hast left us a memorial of Thy Passion ; grant us, we beseech Thee, so to venerate the Sacred Mysteries of Thy Body and Blood, that we may ever feel within ourselves the fruit of Thy Redemption ; who livest and reignest with the FATHER, in the unity of the HOLY SPIRIT, one GOD for ever. *Amen.*

MONDAY, AFTER COMMUNION.

Almighty LORD, who hast given us Thy only begotten SON to take our nature upon Him, and to be born of a pure Virgin ; grant that we, being regenerate and made Thy children by adoption and grace, may daily be renewed by Thy Holy Spirit, through the same our LORD JESUS CHRIST, who liveth and reigneth with Thee and the same Spirit, ever one GOD, world without end. *Amen.*

TUESDAY.

O GOD, who hast prepared for them that love Thee such good things as pass man's understanding, pour into our hearts such love toward Thee that we, loving Thee above all things, may obtain Thy promises, which exceed all that we can desire ; through JESUS CHRIST our Lord. *Amen.*

WEDNESDAY.

LORD of all power and might, who art the Author and Giver of all good things, graft in our hearts the love of Thy Name, increase in us true religion, nourish us with all goodness, and of Thy great mercy keep us in the same ; through JESUS CHRIST our Lord. *Amen.*

Hymns which may fitly be read in preparation or thanksgiving for Holy Communion, or during the celebration itself :

1 BREAD of heaven ! on Thee we feed,
For Thy flesh is meat indeed.
Ever let our souls be fed
With this true and living Bread.
Day by day with strength supplied
Through the life of Him who died.

2 Vine of heaven ! Thy Blood supplies
This blest cup of sacrifice.
LORD ! Thy wounds our healing give ;
To Thy Cross we look, and live.
JESU, may we ever be
Rooted, grafted, built on Thee ! *Amen.*

---

1 DRAW nigh and take the Body of the LORD,
And drink the holy Blood for you outpoured.

2 Saved by that Body and that holy Blood,
With souls refreshed, we render thanks to God.

3 Salvation's Giver, CHRIST, the Only Son,
By His dear Cross and Blood the victory won.

4 Offered was He for greatest and for least,
Himself the Victim, and Himself the Priest.

5 Victims were offered by the law of old,
Which in a type this heavenly mystery told.

6 He, Ransomer from death, and Light from
shade,
Now gives His holy grace His saints to aid.

7 Approach ye then with faithful hearts sincere,
And taste the pledges of salvation here.

8 He, that in this world rules His saints and
shields,
To all believers life eternal yields :

9 With heavenly Bread makes them that hunger
whole,
Gives living Waters to the thirsting soul.

10 O First and Last, to whom all creatures bow,
Our GOD and SAVIOUR, Thou art with us now.
Amen.

1 My God, and is Thy table spread,
   And doth Thy cup with love o'erflow?
   Thither be all Thy children led,
   And let them all Thy sweetness know.

2 Hail, sacred feast, which Jesus makes,
   Rich banquet of His Flesh and Blood !
   Thrice happy he who here partakes
   That sacred stream, that heavenly food.

3 Why are its dainties all in vain
   Before unwilling hearts displayed ?
   Was not for them the Victim slain ?
   Are they forbid the children's bread ?

4 Oh, let Thy table honoured be,
   And furnished well with joyful guests,
   And may each soul salvation see,
   That here its sacred pledges tastes ! *Amen.*

---

1 O God, unseen yet ever near !
   Thy presence may we feel ;
   And thus inspired with holy fear
   Before Thine altar kneel !

2 Here may Thy faithful people know
   The blessings of Thy love ;
   The streams that through the desert flow,
   The manna from above !

3 We come, obedient to Thy word,
   To feast on heavenly food ;
   Our meat the Body of the Lord,
   Our drink His precious Blood.

4 Thus may we all Thy words obey,
   For we, O God, are Thine ;
   And go rejoicing on our way,
   Renewed with strength divine. *Amen.*

1 THEE we adore, O unseen SAVIOUR! Thee,
Who in Thy Feast art pleased with us to be,
Both flesh and spirit at Thy Presence fail,
Yet here Thy Presence we devoutly hail.

2 Oh, blest Memorial of our dying Lord,
Who living Bread to men doth here afford!
Oh, may our souls for ever feed on Thee,
And Thou, O CHRIST, for ever precious be!

3 Fountain of goodness! JESU, LORD and GOD!
Cleanse us, unclean, with Thy most cleansing
      Blood;
Increase our faith and love, that we may know
The hope and peace which from Thy Presence
      flow.

4 O CHRIST! whom now beneath a veil we see,
May what we thirst for soon our portion be;
To gaze on Thee unveiled, and see Thy Face,
The vision of Thy glory and Thy grace. *Amen.*

———

1 WE pray Thee, heavenly FATHER,
      To hear us in Thy love,
And pour upon Thy children
      The unction from above;
That so in love abiding,
      From all defilement free,
We may in pureness offer
      Our Eucharist to Thee.

2 Be Thou our Guide and Helper,
      O JESU CHRIST, we pray;
So may we well approach Thee,
      If Thou wilt be the Way.
Thou, very Truth, hast promised
      To help us in our strife,
Food of the weary pilgrim,
      Eternal Source of Life. *Amen.*

IV.

𝕿𝖍𝖊 𝕾𝖆𝖎𝖑𝖔𝖗'𝖘 𝕷𝖎𝖋𝖊 𝖔𝖋 𝕾𝖔𝖗𝖗𝖔𝖜.

THE season of sickness which seems
to be such a waste of time is really
one which may prove to be of the
greatest value to the Seaman. The
noise of the mess and lower deck is
exchanged for the comparative quiet
of the Sick Bay. The routine of the
ship goes on without him, and he is
relieved, not only from all duty, but
from all anxiety connected with it.
His time and his occupations are for
the most part now his own. The
opportunities which he has looked for
in vain in the season of health are
now presented to him—the opportunities of regular prayer, reading the
Holy Scriptures, self-examination, repentance, resolutions to serve GOD,
preparations for Holy Communion,
and the like. But some have not
sought these opportunities in their
health and so do not welcome them

in sickness. The season of sickness,
therefore, is not only one of opportunity, but one of warning. Sickness
and sorrow are the means by which
GOD tests us—as metals are tested.
According as we are true men, therefore, we shall use this means "to
purify ourselves even as He is pure."
And when sickness or sorrow comes
through our own fault ; through courses
which we can trace, and in which we
have been to blame ; then all the more
it comes to purify us—first, by warning
us of the consequences of sin ; and
afterwards by shewing us, amidst pain
and desolation, how the Blood of
JESUS cleanses us from sin, and re-
stores to us the Life which by sin we
have lost. Let no one, therefore, be
discouraged at the presence of sickness and sorrow. But let no one
either refuse to listen to the stern but
healthful message which they bring.
Many a man has learnt for the first
time in the Sick Bay, his own need
and the preciousness of GOD'S love.
And yet how many a man has passed
through his sickness safely ; has been

healed by the surgeon of his bodily plague, but has returned to his duty with his heart still hardened, and the disease of his soul nothing bettered, but rather grown worse! To such an one, sickness and sorrow—however and wherever they have come—have been indeed a sad waste of time.

The following prayers and suggestions are intended to prevent this, and to provide the Seaman with something which will enable him to understand better the reason of the Chaplain's visits to the Sick Bay ; or, if there be no Chaplain, something which will speak in his ear a word for GOD, at a time when he ought to be most inclined to listen.

If a man has been brought into the Sick List through intemperance or impurity of life, or if he neglects private prayer, let him read the following words of GOD :—

" Seek ye the LORD, while He may be found :

Call ye upon Him while He is near.

Let the wicked forsake his way, and the unrighteous man his thoughts :

Let him return unto the LORD, and He will have mercy upon him ;

And to our GOD, for He will abundantly pardon."—*Isaiah* lv. 6, 7.

" Behold I stand at the door and knock : if any man hear My voice, and open the door, I will come in to him, and will sup with him, and he with Me."—*Revelation* iii. 20.

PRAYERS TO BE SAID DAILY AFTER THOSE ON pp. 12, etc.

Psalm cxxx. *De profundis.*

Out of the deep have I called unto Thee, O LORD ; LORD, hear my voice.

O let Thine ears consider well the voice of my complaint.

If Thou, LORD, wilt be extreme to mark what is done amiss ; O LORD, . who may abide it ?

For there is mercy with Thee, therefore shalt Thou be feared.

I look for the LORD ; my soul doth wait· for Him ; in His word is my trust.

My soul fleeth unto the LORD ; before the morning watch, I say, before the morning watch.

O Israel, trust in the LORD, for with the LORD there is mercy, and with Him is plenteous redemption.

And He shall redeem Israel from all his sins.

Glory be to the FATHER, &c.

LORD, have mercy, &c.

Our FATHER, &c.

O most Mighty GOD and Merciful Father, who dost correct those whom Thou dost love, and in very faithfulness dost afflict the children of men; I pray Thee to give me grace patiently to bear the sufferings which Thou hast seen fit to lay upon me, and to submit myself wholly to Thy will.

O LORD, in the midst of judgment Thou hast remembered Mercy. I thank Thee that while thousands fall around me, Thou hast yet spared my life, and given me hopes of recovery, and longer service to Thy glory upon earth. Help me to spend the remainder of my days in Thy faith and fear; that, this life ended, I may dwell with Thee in life everlasting; through JESUS CHRIST our Lord. *Amen.*

O Almighty GOD, whose most

dearly beloved SON for the forgiveness of our sins did shed out of His most Precious Side both Water and Blood; grant me without all doubt to believe in Thy SON JESUS CHRIST, and to look unto Him for pardon and peace; that I may be cleansed from all my sins, and serve Thee with a quiet mind; through the same Thy Blessed SON. *Amen.*

O Saviour of the world, who by Thy Cross and Precious Blood hast redeemed us, save me and help me, I humbly beseech Thee, O LORD.

SHORT PRAYERS.

To be said by the Sick and the Wounded, as opportunity may offer.

We adore Thee, O CHRIST, and we bless Thee, who, by Thy Cross and Passion, hast redeemed the world.

O JESUS, Saviour of sinners, by that unjust sentence of death pronounced against Thee, deliver me from the sentence of eternal death which my sins have so justly deserved.

O JESUS, Saviour of sinners, who

didst voluntarily take upon Thyself the heavy Cross of my sins, make me feel their heavy weight, and make me heartily sorry for them the remainder of my life.

O JESUS, Saviour of sinners, who didst voluntarily take on Thyself the shame and confusion of my sins, make me to be ashamed and confounded for them.

O JESUS, Saviour of sinners, who didst voluntarily die a painful and a shameful death, grant me to die to sin, and to live to Thee.

O JESUS, Saviour of sinners, who didst voluntarily suffer shame and torture for us, make me to suffer patiently for love of Thee.

O JESUS, Saviour of sinners, and Captain of our salvation, who wast made perfect through suffering, correct me here, and spare me in eternity.

LORD, remember me when Thou comest into Thy kingdom. I believe in Thee, O LORD, but may I believe. more firmly. I hope in Thee, O LORD, but may I hope more fully. I love Thee, O LORD, but may I love more ardently. I grieve that I have offended Thee, O LORD, but may I grieve more sincerely.

I adore Thee, as my first beginning. I long after Thee, as my last end. I praise Thee, as my ceaseless Benefactor. I call upon Thee, as my Refuge and my Defence.

Direct me by Thy wisdom, protect me by Thy power, comfort me by Thy mercy, and save me by Thy love.

I pray Thee, O LORD, to enlighten my understanding, to direct my will, to purify my body, and to sanctify my soul.

May I bewail my past sins, resist future temptations, correct vicious desires, and cultivate all virtues.

Grant me, O LORD, the love of Thee, distrust of myself, zeal for my neighbour, and contempt of the world.

Grant me earnestness in prayer, moderation in food, and firmness in my resolves.

Teach me, O LORD, the nothingness of this world, the greatness of Heaven, the shortness of time, and the length of eternity.

Grant that I may
   Prepare for Death :
   Fear the Judgment:
   Escape Hell :
   Obtain Heaven.
And this I pray through JESUS CHRIST our Lord. *Amen.*

Prayer which may be said before an Operation.

" O cast thy burden upon the LORD, and He shall refresh thee : and will not suffer the righteous to fall for ever."
 LORD, have mercy upon me.
 CHRIST, have mercy upon me.
 LORD, have mercy upon me.
 Our FATHER, &c.
 O most merciful FATHER, who rulest all things by the counsel of Thy will, whose hand can wound and heal, who dost bring to the grave, and restorest again to life ; I bow myself before Thee, O LORD, and beseech Thee to be merciful unto me, to pardon all my sins, and to preserve me in this hour of danger. Grant me grace patiently to take the sufferings which Thou hast

laid upon me, and do Thou support
me in my weakness. LORD, Thou
knowest whereof we are made : Thou
rememberest that we are but dust ;
Thou givest power to the faint, and to
them that have no might Thou in-
creasest strength. Grant that, waiting
upon Thee, I may renew my strength,
and believe that all things work together for good to them that love God.
Give me courage bravely to endure
whatever pain I may yet have to
undergo, as a good Soldier of JESUS
CHRIST. *Amen.*

Prayer which may be said when in
Severe Suffering.

O LORD JESU CHRIST, the only Son
of God, who wast given to be a sacrifice for sin, and hast also left us a perfect example of patient suffering, even
unto death ; give me grace to follow
Thy example in all things, and patiently
to bear the Cross Thou hast laid upon
me. Conform Thy servant to the likeness of Thy Passion ; subdue in me all
murmuring against Thy will, all fret-
fulness and discontent. Teach me to

endure hardness as a good Soldier of Thy cross; and grant that, cleansed from my sins in Thy Blood, and trusting wholly in Thee, by the merits of Thy Death and Passion, I may be admitted hereafter into Thine eternal kingdom, to praise Thee for ever. *Amen.*

Short Sentences when in great Pain.

O comfort the soul of Thy servant :

For unto Thee, O LORD, do I lift up my soul.

Hear me, O LORD, and that soon, for my spirit waxeth faint :

Hide not Thy face from me, lest I be like unto them that go down into the pit.

My heart and my flesh faileth :

But GOD is the strength of my life, and my portion for ever.

Why art thou so vexed, O my soul :

Why art thou so disquieted within me ?

O put thou thy trust in GOD,

For I will yet thank Him, which is the help of my countenance.

O LORD JESU CHRIST, who for the

salvation of the world wast willing to
bear patiently sorrow and agony, passion and death ; grant that, mindful of
Thy patience in all that Thou hast
borne for us, we may bear our light
affliction patiently for Thy sake ; that
so, sharing in Thy sorrow, we may become partakers of Thy glory : who
livest and reignest with the FATHER
and the HOLY SPIRIT, one GOD, world
without end. *Amen.*

THOUGHTS FOR THE SICK AND WOUNDED.

"Surely He hath borne our griefs,
and carried our sorrows. . . . He was
wounded for our transgressions. He
was bruised for our iniquity."—*Isaiah*
liii. 4, 5.

"If, when ye do well, and suffer for
it, ye take it patiently, this is acceptable with GOD.

"For even hereunto were ye called ;
because CHRIST also suffered for us,
leaving us an example, that ye should
follow His steps : who did no sin,
neither was guile found in His mouth :
who, when He was reviled, reviled

not again; when He suffered He threatened not; but committed Himself to Him that judgeth righteously:

"Who His own self bare our sins in His own Body on the tree [upon the Cross],

"That we, being dead to sins, should live unto righteousness:

"By whose stripes ye were healed."
—1 *Peter* ii. 20–24.

"It became Him, for whom are all things, and by whom are all things, in bringing many sons unto glory, to make the Captain of their salvation perfect through sufferings."—*Hebrews* ii. 10.

"Looking unto JESUS the Author and Finisher of our faith; who for the joy that was set before Him endured the Cross, despising the shame, and is set down at the right hand of the throne of GOD."—*Hebrew* xii. 2.

"He that overcometh shall not be hurt of the second death. And I will grant unto him to sit with Me in My throne, even as I also overcame, and am set down with My FATHER in His throne."—*Revelation* ii. 11, iii. 21.

"Be thou faithful unto death ; and I will give thee a Crown of Life."—*Revelation* ii. 10.

FOR ONE TROUBLED IN MIND.

Hear what comfortable words our Saviour CHRIST saith unto all that truly turn to Him :—

"Come unto Me, all ye that travail and are heavy laden, and I will refresh you."—*Matthew* xi. 28.

"GOD so loved the world, that He gave His only begotten SON, to the end that all that believe in Him should not perish, but have everlasting life."—*John* iii. 16.

"This is a true saying, and worthy of all men to be received, that CHRIST JESUS came into the world to save sinners."—1 *Timothy* i. 15.

"If any man sin, we have an Advocate with the FATHER, JESUS CHRIST the righteous : and He is the propitiation for our sins."—1 *John* ii. 1, 2.

"If we confess our sins, He is faithful and just to forgive us our sins, and to cleanse us from all unrighteousness."—1 *John* i. 9.

"Beloved, *now* are we the sons of GOD; and . . . we know that, when He shall appear, we shall be like Him; for we shall see Him as He is."— 1 *John* iii. 2.

"He is our peace; in whom we have Redemption through His Blood, even the forgiveness of sins."—*Ephesians* ii. 14; *Colossians* i. 14.

Prayer.

O LORD JESU, who after Thy Resurrection didst manifest Thyself to Thy Disciples, giving them peace and the HOLY GHOST; grant unto me Thy servant that peace which the world cannot give. Grant me Thy grace that I may cling trustfully to Thee in joy and in sorrow, and be faithful unto death. Teach me to love Thee, fear Thee, praise Thee, and adore Thee. And since Thou alone knowest what is good for us, do Thou order my life and being, my words and deeds, as may best promote Thy glory and my salvation; who livest and reignest with the FATHER and the HOLY GHOST, ever one GOD, world without end. *Amen.*

PRAYERS FOR A DYING SEAMAN.

These devotions are divided into short portions to be used as opportunity may offer. They are not intended to supersede those in the Prayer Book, which the Christian Seaman will always have with him : and which the Chaplain will in most cases be at hand to offer for him. Let him consider thoughtfully what the Church has said in Her office " for the Visitation of the Sick," as to confession in the case of those who feel their consciences to be troubled with any weighty matter, and as to ministerial absolution, at this solemn moment. If he is unable to read, a messmate can select portions, as most suitable to read for him.

LORD, have mercy upon me.

CHRIST, have mercy upon me.

LORD, have mercy upon me.

Our FATHER, &c.

O Holy FATHER, who didst so love the world as to give Thine only begotten SON, that whosoever believeth in Him should not perish, but have everlasting life,

Have mercy upon me, a sinner.

O Blessed JESU, who didst taste death for all men, and hast promised to .accept all such as come to Thee, cast me not away from Thee, but

Have mercy upon me, a sinner.

O Blessed SPIRIT, whose sacred fires melt the hardest heart, who leadest sinners to repentance, and art the Comforter of the sad and wounded soul, do Thou guide me, keep me, comfort me, and

Have mercy upon me, a sinner.

O ever blessed TRINITY, in whose image we were created, restore in me that heavenly likeness, and

Have mercy upon me, a sinner.

PRAYERS TO JESUS FOR PARDON.

O LORD JESUS CHRIST, Saviour of the world, who mercifully invitest sinners to Thy Cross, that they may be cleansed from their sin ; I come to Thee, whom my sins have pierced, humbly believing that Thou art able and most willing to receive me, and wilt wash away the guilt and stains of my past sinful life, and make me clean.

Look upon me, O LORD, as Thou didst on the penitent thief, and have mercy on me ; and as Thou, of very love, didst pray for Thy murderers, do. Thou intercede for me, that Thy blessed Passion, and all-sufficient Sacrifice, may atone for my offences.

Receive me, O Thou loving Shepherd of souls, receive me, Thy poor wandering sheep. Let not my soul be lost, which Thou didst come down from heaven to save.

"LORD, into Thy hands I commend myself, for Thou hast redeemed me, O LORD, Thou GOD of Truth."

O LORD JESU CHRIST, who didst stretch out Thine hands on the Cross, and redeem us by Thy Blood ; forgive me, a sinner, for none of my thoughts are hid from Thee. Pardon I ask, pardon I hope for, pardon I trust to find : for Thou art the GOD of mercy, and with Thee is plenteous Redemption.

O Saviour of the world, who by Thy Cross and precious Blood hast redeemed us, save us and help us, we humbly beseech Thee, O LORD.

LITANY OF THE PASSION.

O merciful JESU, my LORD and my GOD,

By the Meekness and Lowliness of Thy suffering Life ;

By the unknown Sorrows of Thine Agony and Bloody Sweat ;

By the Buffetings and Scourging ;

By Thy Crown of Thorns ;

By Thy Hands and Feet nailed through ;

By Thy pierced Side ;

By Thine awful Thirst and bitter Cry ;

By Thy Body broken,

By Thy Blood poured out,

Have mercy upon me.

By Thy words of mercy on the Cross, Thy promise to the penitent, Thy prayer for Thy murderers,

Have mercy upon me.

By Thy Bowing of the Head, and Thy giving up the Ghost,

Have mercy upon me.

LORD, remember me when Thou comest into Thy Kingdom.

O Lamb of GOD, that takest away
the sin of the world,

Have mercy upon me.

O Lamb of GOD, that takest away
the sin of the world,

Grant me Thy Peace.

O Blessed JESU, who hast loved
me, and washed me from my sins in
Thine own Blood, receive my soul
when it departs from the body into the
joyful abodes of Thine elect, to dwell
for ever in Thy glorious Presence.

O Blessed JESU, who by death
didst take away the sting of death,
and by Thy Resurrection hast opened
to us the gate of Everlasting Life;
grant unto me that, wholly trusting in
Thy mercy, I may fall asleep peace-
fully in Thee, and awaking up after
Thy likeness, may be admitted to the
joys of Paradise to praise Thee eter-
nally.

" Behold, I come quickly."

" Even so, come, LORD JESUS."

CONSOLATION FOR A DYING SEAMAN ALARMED ON ACCOUNT OF SIN.

Question. Dost thou believe that the LORD JESUS CHRIST died for thee ?

Answer. I believe it.

Question. Dost thou thank Him for His Passion and Death ?

Answer. I do thank Him.

Question. Dost thou believe that thou canst not be saved except by His Death ?

Answer. I believe it.

Come, then, Christian Seaman, while life remains to thee ; in His Death alone place thy whole trust ; trust in nothing else ; to His Death commit thyself entirely ; let it be thy entire protection. And if the LORD thy GOD will judge thee, say, "O LORD, between me and Thy judgment I offer the Death of our LORD JESUS CHRIST ; otherwise I cannot stand before Thee." And if He shall say that thou art a sinner, say thou, "O LORD, I put the Death of our LORD JESUS CHRIST between my sins and Thee." If He say that thou hast deserved condemnation, say, "LORD, I place the Death of our LORD JESUS CHRIST between the evils I have deserved and Thee; His merits I offer for those I ought to have, and have not." If He say that He is angry with thee, say, "LORD, let the Death of JESUS CHRIST be a shield between Thy wrath and me." And when thou hast finished, say again, "LORD, I set the Death of JESUS CHRIST, my Saviour, between Thee and me."

ON THE APPROACH OF DEATH.

It is imperative upon a dying Seaman to receive the Holy Communion, if possible; and no one at such a time would neglect so important a duty, and so great a blessing and comfort. The Christian Seaman will do what he believes CHRIST has commanded; and if he feel his conscience troubled with any weighty matter, and if he humbly and heartily desire it, his appointed Minister will absolve him on confession of his sins, as His Church directs in the Office of Visitation of the Sick. If no Priest be near him, he will use some of the prayers in Chapter iii. of this book, and the Litany of the Passion ; or a messmate will read them for him. Also, as opportunity serves, let him read or have read to him the following :

Psalm cxxx. (p. 94.)

LORD, have mercy upon me ;
CHRIST, have mercy upon me ;
LORD, have mercy upon me ;
Our FATHER, &c.

" In the midst of life we are in death; of whom may we seek for succour but of Thee, O LORD, who for our sins art justly displeased?

" Yet, O LORD GOD most Holy, O LORD most Mighty, O Holy and most Merciful Saviour, deliver me not into the bitter pains of eternal death.

" Thou knowest, LORD, the secrets of the heart ; shut not Thy merciful ears to my prayer : but spare me, O LORD most Holy, O GOD most Mighty, O Holy and Merciful Saviour, Thou most Worthy Judge eternal, suffer me not at my last hour to fall from Thee !"

O Holy JESU, Saviour of sinners, who by Thy Precious Death hast

8

atoned for sin, and by Thy Resurrection hast overcome Death, and opened unto us the gate of Everlasting Life ; I pray Thee to have mercy upon me. LORD, wash my soul from every stain of sin ; sprinkle me with Thy precious Blood. Hide me in Thy pierced Side ; carry me safely through the Dark Valley.

Look on me as Thou didst look in infinite compassion on the penitent thief, and remember me, LORD, when Thou comest into Thy Kingdom.

Thou, O LORD, hast redeemed me ; suffer not that to be lost which Thou hast redeemed.

LORD, for me Thou didst pay the price with Thy most Precious Blood ; suffer not that to be cast away, which Thou hast bought so dearly.

LORD, Thou hast made me in Thine Own Image ; Suffer not Thine Image to be blotted out.

LORD, into Thy hands I commend myself, as unto a faithful Creator, and most Merciful Father.

O Blessed JESU, my LORD and my GOD, who hast loved me, and washed

me from my sins in Thine Own Blood,
receive my soul into the joyful abode
of Thine elect, to dwell for ever in
Thy glorious Presence.

In the hour of death, in the day of
judgment,

Good LORD, deliver me.

That when my soul shall depart
from the body, its place may be in
peace, its abode in Paradise ;

Hear me, O JESU, my Saviour.

That the light of Thy Love may
sustain and comfort me in my last
conflict ;

Hear me, O JESU, my Saviour.

That Holy Angels may conduct my
soul into Thy Presence, and that it
may be accepted through Thine own
infinite merits ;

Hear me, O JESU, my Saviour.

That Thou mayest receive me as
Thy faithful Soldier and servant into
the joy of my LORD ;

Hear me, O JESU, my Saviour.

O Lamb of GOD, that takest away the sin of the world,

Have mercy upon me.

O Lamb of GOD, that takest away the sin of the world,

Grant me Thy Peace.

A PRAYER WHICH MAY BE SAID ON THE DEATH OF A SHIPMATE.

O remember how short my time is;
Wherefore hast Thou made all men for nought?
When Thou hidest Thy face they are troubled.
When Thou takest away their breath they die, and are turned again to their dust.
So teach us to number our days,
That we may apply our hearts unto wisdom.
"Watch therefore, for ye know neither the day, nor the hour, wherein the SON of MAN cometh."—*Matthew* xxv. 13.

Prayer.[1]

O GOD, who hast appointed unto us all once to die, but hast mercifully concealed from us the hour of our death; grant me so to profit by this Thy visitation, that I may redeem the time Thou yet givest me. Help me now, amidst health and strength, in the duties and trials of life, to remember Thee, to fear, and honour Thee. Fit and prepare me for my last hour; and grant me so to live as a faithful Soldier of the Cross, in holiness and righteousness all my days, that I may die happily in Thy love, and attain everlasting Life, through JESUS CHRIST. *Amen.*

ON RECOVERY FROM SICKNESS.

The best way in which the Christian Seaman can render thanks to GOD for His mercy in giving him back his life, is to give himself up to His service, "*to offer the Service of Thanksgiving*" (*i.e.*, Eucharist), and receive the

---

[1] If this Prayer is used in the Sick Bay, and said aloud, change "me" and "I" into "us" and "we."

sacrament of the blessed Body and Blood of CHRIST, as He has commanded. He will not forget, too, to give something to the Church at the Offertory, as a proof of his thankfulness.

"What reward shall I give unto the LORD: for all the benefits He hath done unto me?

"I will receive the Cup of Salvation: and call upon the name of the LORD."

O most gracious GOD, I humbly beseech Thee to accept this my most hearty praise and thanksgiving for this Thy great goodness vouchsafed to me. LORD, I am unworthy of the least of Thy mercies. "Praise the LORD, O my soul; and all that is within me bless His Holy Name. Who has saved my life from destruction, and crowneth me with mercy and loving-kindness." Grant me now to go forth to my daily duties resolved to confess Thee before men, and in the faithful discharge of my duties to render Thee unceasing and devoted service. Do Thou enable me, O LORD JESUS, to continue Thy faithful Sailor and Servant, unto my life's end. *Amen.*

"Watch ye : stand fast in the faith : Quit you like men : be strong."—1 *Corinthians* xvi. 13.

Be careful that this thanksgiving or one like it is used after you are discharged from Hospital or the Sick List, as well as when you have begun to recover. We are very apt to thank GOD with our lips in the quiet of the Sick Bay, but to forget to shew forth our thankfulness by our lives when we have returned to our mess and our duty.

Psalms and Passages from Holy Scripture for the Sick and Sorrowful.

In Sorrow for Sin :—*Psalm* vi., xvi., xix., xxiii., xxv., xxxii., xxxviii., xxxix., li., lv., lxi., lxii., cii., cxxx., cxxxix., cxlii., clxiii.

Recovery from Sickness :—*Psalm* xxvii., xxx., xxxi., xl.

Thanksgiving :—*Psalm* xxxiv., lx., lxi., lxii., ciii., cxxi.

For Encouragement:—*Psalm* xxxvii.

In Heaviness:—*Psalm* lxii., lxix., lxx., lxxvii., lxxxiv., lxxxvi.

Praise :—*Psalm* lxiii.

In Great Trouble :—*Psalm* lxxxviii., lc.; *Isaiah* liv. 2–10.   *The Book of the Lamentations of Jeremiah.*   1 *Corinthians* xv.; 2 *Corinthians* iv. 16 to v. 9; *Luke* xvi. 19–31; *John* xi.; *Isaiah* liii.'; *Romans* viii. 8–39; 1 *Thessalonians* iv.; 1 *Peter* i.; *Isaiah* xl.; *Philippians* iii.; *Job* xxxiii.; *James* v.; *John* xiv., xv., xvi.; *Revelation* vii. 9–17; *Matthew* i., xxv.; *Luke* xii.; *Ecclesiastes* xii.; 1 *Peter* ii.; *Job* v.; 2 *Samuel* xxi.; *Psalm* cxix., lxxi.

If a seaman by any just impediment do not receive the Sacrament of CHRIST'S Body and Blood, let him be assured that "if he do truly repent him of his sins, and stedfastly believe that JESUS CHRIST hath suffered death upon the cross for him, and shed His Blood for his redemption, earnestly remembering the benefits he hath thereby, and giving Him hearty thanks therefore, he doth eat and drink the Body and Blood of our Saviour CHRIST profitably to his soul's health, although he do not receive the Sacrament with his mouth." (From the Prayer Book.)

V.

The Sailor's Life of Love.

LOVE TO GOD.

"THOU shalt love the LORD thy GOD with all thy heart, and with all thy soul, and with all thy mind."—*Matthew* xxii. 37.

The Seaman should aim at making these words of the Psalmist true of himself. "Thy words have I hid within my heart that I should not sin against Thee:" or these others, "Wherewithal shall a young man cleanse his way? even by ruling himself after Thy Word." Considering that every boy before he leaves the training-ship has a present made him of a Bible and Prayer Book, and that in every ship the Admiralty places a large number of these books for the use of the ship's company, it would seem that the Seaman had every opportunity given him of so studying the Word of GOD as to be, indeed, able to "hide it within his heart," where it *must* get before it can do good to any man. And so it is. Whatever difficulties there are in the way of the regular study of God's Word are certainly not placed there by our rulers. But unless the Seaman does make a habit of reading his Bible, he cannot expect to know anything of that hidden meaning which GOD gives to those who have learnt to place it reverently, carefully, and frequently in their heart. How shall he "cleanse his way," if he is not continually "ruling himself after GOD'S Word?" "The words of the LORD are pure words," and that is just why they have such a cleansing power, that by them we can discern the difference between the pathway of holiness and the broad, muddy road of sin. There is so much room in the one, sin abounds so plentifully on every side, that it is often very diffi-cult for the Seaman to distinguish the "narrow way" which leads to eternal life. But GOD will shew it to him who loves His Word.

Does he want the courage or the inclination to sit down in his mess, and read his Bible? If it is courage he lacks, what will he do when he comes to die? Will he have courage *then?* If it is inclination that is wanting, he is indeed in a bad way; for if he is not inclined to read GOD's Word, he will not be inclined to keep them, and then, GOD help him! for man cannot.

It is a good thing for a Seaman to read his Bible every day, if it be only one verse. In the dinner hour anywhere but in the mess, in the mess during the watch below, on the forecastle in the last "dog," during the stray minutes which can so easily be picked up when waiting for divisions, &c.—here are times when *no* work is going on and when so many men are simply idle. But, again, let him not stow himself away. The Seaman is to let his light shine before men, which does not mean that he is to "wave it about," as has been said, but quietly to let it shine in the places which have been given him to live in. He will soon learn to hear GOD's words

above the racket of the mess, above
the idle jèst and wicked blasphemy.
But he must be in earnest, and he
must be a little brave, only a little,
for the difficulty from his shipmates
will be much less than he supposes.

It is a good thing to have a routine
for the study of the Bible, a routine
even if we have time for no more than a
verse.   Let a man secure his verse in
the early part of the day if possible,
and then if more time is given him he
can go on with his chapter.   And
what chapter shall it be? It is unwise
to have no system, to open the Book
at haphazard.   This may do for one
who seldom reads, but not for one
who wants to *study* the Word of GOD.

No better rule can be adopted than
that laid down in the Calendar of the
Prayer Book, where for every day in
the year four portions of Holy Scripture are given, from which he may
make a choice, and by which he will
be able to read the greater part of the
Bible through in the year.   He will
never be at a loss then where to turn
for his daily passage.   Again, the

Book of Psalms will give him great comfort and instruction. The following is a table which provides a Psalm or a portion of a Psalm for every day in the month.

DAY. PSALM.

1. i.; iii.; iv.; vi. 6, 7, 8, 12, 13; viii.
2. ix. 1–5, 7–12; xi.; xiii.
3. xv.; xvi.; xvii. 1–9, 16; xviii. 1–7, 30–37, 47.
4. xix.; xx.; xxii.; xxiii.
5. xxiv.; xxv. 1–21; xxvii. 1–6.
6. xxx. 1–13; xxxi. 1–7; xxxi. 16 to end; xxxii.; xxxiii. 11 to end.
7. xxxv. 1–18; xxxvi.; xxxvii. 1–12, and 23–33; and 35 to end.
8. xxxviii.; xxxix.; xl.; xli.; xlii.; xliii.;
9. xliv. 1–10; xliv. 16 to end; xlvi.; xlviii.; xlix. 6–3, and 15 to end.
10. l. 14 to end; li.; liii.; liv. 17–23.
11. lvi.; lvii. 6 to end; lix.
12. lxii.; lxiii.; lxv.; lxvi. 1–9, and 14 to end.
13. lxviii. 1–11, and 32 to end; lxix. 13–22, and 30 to end; lxx.
14. lxxi. 1–9, and 13–20; lxxiii.; lxxiv. 17 to end.

DAY.	PSALM.
15.	lxxvi. 6 to end ; lxxvii. 5–14.
16.	lxxx. 3–8, or 7 to end ; lxxxi. 9 to end ; lxxxii. ; lxxxiv. ; lxxxv.
17.	lxxxvi. 1–11, and 11 to end ; lxxxviii. ; lxxxix. 1–10.
18.	xc. ; xci. ; xcii. ; xciii. ; xciv. 12–22.
19.	xcv. ; xcvii.
20.	ciii. 1–7, or 8–14 ; civ. 24–33.
21.	cv. 1–8.
22.	cvii. 1–10, or 23–32 ; cviii. 1–13.
23.	cxiii. ; cxiv. 12 to end.
24.	cxvi. ; cxviii. ; any portion of cxix. to ver. 33.
25.	Any portion of cxix. between ver. 33 and ver. 105.
26.	Any portion of cxix. between ver. 105 and end.
27.	cxx. ; cxxi. ; cxxii. ; cxxiii. ; cxxiv. ; cxxv. ; cxxvi. ; cxxvii. ; cxxviii. ; cxxix. ; cxxx. ; cxxxi.
28.	cxxxv. 1–7 ; cxxxviii.
29.	cxxxix. 1–12, or 13–19 ; cxli. 1–9 ; cxliii. 1–11.
30.	cxliv. 1–10 ; cxlv. 1–10, or 10 to end ; cxlvi.
31.	cxlvii. 1–8, or 11 to end ; cxlviii. ; cxlix.

Prayer Book Collects suitable for various needs.

Benefits of the
  death of Christ. The Annunciation.
Imitation of Christ 2nd. S. aft. Easter.
The Church and
  Clergy ... ... Ember Collects, 3rd
                     S. in Advent; 5th,
                     16th, 22nd S. after
                     Trinity.
Sorrow for Sin ... Ash Wednesday
Conversion of
  Heathen ... ... 3rd Coll. for Good
                     Friday.
Christian Courage. St. John Baptist.
Faith ... ... Trinity Sunday,
                     14th S. after Trin-
                     ity, St. Thomas.
Final Blessedness. St. John Evang.
                     Epiphany. S. after
                     Ascension Day. All
                     Saints.
Guidance and
  Grace ... ... 4th S. in Advent;
                     Christmas Day;
                     1st S. after Epi-
                     phany; 5th S. in
                     Lent; Easter

Day; 5th S. after Easter. 1st, 4th, 9th, 11th, 13th, 17th, 19th, 25th S. after Trinity.

Heavenly Minded-
ness ...   . 4th S. after Easter. Ascension Day.

Help in Trouble or
Danger   ...   ... Collects in Litany : 3rd and 4th S. after Epiphany, 2nd and 3rd S. in Lent, 2nd, 3rd, 8th, 15th, 20th S. after Trinity.

Love   ...   . St. Stephen, Quin-quagesima.

Love of God...   ... 6th and 7th S. after Trinity.

Love of God's Word 2nd S. in Advent. St. Paul. St. Luke.

Pardon ...   . Septuagesima. 4th S. in Lent, 12th, 21st, 24th S. after Trinity.

Patience   ...   ... 6th S. in Lent.

Peace   ...   . 2nd S. after Epiph-any.

Perseverance ... 3rd S. after Easter.
Prayer, Answer to 10th and 23rd S. after Trinity.
Preparation for
Judgment... ... 1st and 3rd S. in Advent.
Purity of heart and
life ... ... Holy Innocents; Circumcision; 6th S. after Epiphany; 1st S. in Lent; Easter Eve; 1st S. after Easter; 18th S. after Trinity; Purification; St. James.
Readiness of Will. St. Andrew.
Unworldliness ... St. Matthew.

LOVE TO MAN.

" Thou shalt love thy neighbour as thyself."—*Matthew* xxii. 39.

" I exhort that, first of all supplications, prayers, intercessions, and giving of thanks be made for all men ; for kings and for all that are in authority ; that we may lead a quiet and peace-

able life in all godliness and honesty."
—1 *Timothy* ii. 1, 2.

For the Church.

Almighty and Everlasting GOD, by whose Spirit the whole body of the Church is governed and sanctified, receive our supplications and prayers which we offer before Thee for all estates of men in Thy Holy Church, that every member of the same in his vocation and ministry may truly and godly serve Thee; through our Lord and Saviour JESUS CHRIST. *Amen.*

For the Queen.

Good LORD, I beseech Thee to keep and strengthen in the true worshipping of Thee, in righteousness and holiness of life, Thy servant Victoria our Queen. Rule her heart in Thy faith, fear, and love, that she may evermore trust in Thee, and ever seek Thy honour and glory; through JESUS CHRIST our Lord. *Amen.*

For the Commanding Officer.

Bless, O GOD, Thy servant whom Thou hast placed in command of this ship. Let Thy Holy Spirit guide him in all his undertakings, and help him in the anxieties of his office. Enable him so to serve Thee in this life that, finally, he may be brought to Thine everlasting kingdom ; through JESUS CHRIST our Lord. *Amen.*

For Officers.

Pour Thy blessing, O LORD, on the officers of this ship : especially [*here mention any you want to pray for by name*], that they may rule themselves and us in Thy fear and love ; grant that the obedience which we render to them may be ready and sincere. Fill them with the spirit of wisdom, courage, and of a right mind, that with hearts devoted to Thee they may perform their several duties to Thy honour and glory, and to the edification of all men ; through JESUS CHRIST our Lord. *Amen.*

For the Chaplain.

O LORD JESU CHRIST, who at Thy first coming didst send Thy messenger to prepare Thy way before Thee, grant that the Chaplains of the Fleet, and especially [*here mention your own Chaplain's name*], may likewise so prepare and make ready Thy way, by turning the hearts of the disobedient to the wisdom of the just, that at Thy second coming to judge the world we may be found an acceptable people in Thy sight, who livest and reignest with the FATHER and the HOLY SPIRIT, ever one GOD, world without end. *Amen.*

For the Scripture Reader.

Blessed LORD, who hast caused all Holy Scriptures to be written for our learning, grant that in the reading of them by Thy servant, the Scripture Reader, we may in such wise hear them, read, mark, learn, and inwardly digest them, that by patience and comfort of Thy Holy Word we may embrace and ever hold fast the blessed hope of everlasting life, which Thou hast given us in our Saviour JESUS CHRIST. *Amen.*

For an Unhappy Ship

O GOD, who makest men to be of one mind in a house, mercifully put to flight the causes of our dissensions, and grant us to serve Thee in the unity of the Spirit and the bond of peace ; through JESUS CHRIST our Lord. *Amen.*

For a Happy Ship.

Grant, O LORD, that the peace and contentment that, by Thy mercy, we enjoy in this ship, may teach us, by Thy mercy, to seek after that peace which passeth all understanding ; through JESUS CHRIST our Lord. *Amen.*

For the Service.

O Eternal LORD GOD, who alone spreadest out the heavens and rulest the raging of the sea, who hast compassed the water with bounds until day and night come to an end ; be pleased to receive into Thy almighty and most gracious protection the persons of us Thy servants and the Fleet in which we serve. Preserve us from the dangers of the sea and from the violence of the enemy ; that we may be a safeguard unto our most gracious Sovereign Lady Queen Victoria and her dominions, and a security for such as pass on the seas upon their lawful occasions, that the inhabitants of our Island may serve Thee, our GOD; through JESUS CHRIST our Lord. *Amen.*

For our Parents.

O LORD, have mercy upon my [father and mother], and bless *them*; giving *them* all things needful whether for soul or body; through JESUS CHRIST our Lord. *Amen.*

For a Wife.

O LORD, bless my wife, and give her grace faithfully to perform all that belongs to her position. Help me in my duties towards her, that I may be a comfort and support to her by affectionate counsel and diligent labour. Amend what is amiss in either of us, and grant that we may assist one another to advance in holiness, so that our love may be made perfect by Thy blessing; through JESUS CHRIST our Lord. *Amen.*

For Children.

Almighty GOD and Heavenly FATHER, I thank Thee for the child [*or* children] which Thou hast given me ; give me also grace to train *him* in Thy faith, fear, and love, that as *he* advances in years *he* may grow in grace, and may hereafter be found in the number of Thine elect children ; through JESUS CHRIST our Lord. *Amen.*

For Brothers and Sisters.

O Heavenly FATHER, strengthen me and my [brothers and sisters] in the holy bonds of Thy love, by drawing us all to an increasing love of Thyself, till the brotherhood which has begun upon earth shall be perfected in Thy heavenly kingdom ; through JESUS CHRIST our Lord. *Amen.*

For any Relative or Friend who has shewn us kindness.

O GOD, who hast put it into the heart of my [*here mention the relation and name*] to shew kindness to me ; and, whether I am on board or ashore, to bear me in *his* heart, mercifully reward *him* sevenfold, and give us both grace so to be joined together in love for Thee, that, loving Thee above all things, we may obtain Thy gracious promises, which exceed all that we can desire ; through JESUS CHRIST our Lord. *Amen.*

For Friends at Home.

Be gracious, O LORD, to all my friends and acquaintances at home, and grant that all our dealings with each other, whether by letter or by thought, may be hallowed by the guidance, and prospered through the intercession, of Thy SON JESUS CHRIST our Lord. *Amen.*

For a Sweetheart.

Grant, O LORD, that she whom Thou hast given me to share my heart and affections may ever be protected by the angel of Thy Providence. Defend her in all temptations. Strengthen her in all good resolves and intentions. Keep her faithful to me, and me to her, and both of us to Thee, that united now in love, we may in Thy good time be united in marriage, and serve Thee faithfully all the days of our life ; through JESUS CHRIST our Lord. *Amen.*

Another.

O GOD, who makest all things work together for good to them that love Thee, dispose the heart of Thy servant [*here mention her*] to love Thee more and more ; and give us grace to love each other in Thee and for Thee. Grant us so to order our thoughts and desires concerning things earthly, that loving Thee more than all else, we may both at last attain to the fulness of Thy love in heaven ; through JESUS CHRIST our Lord. *Amen.*

For a Chum.

Grant, O LORD, to my chum [*here mention him*] the grace of Thy Holy Spirit, that He may in all things please Thee ; and let the assistance which we render to each other in things earthly teach us to be fellow-workers together in things heavenly, to Thy honour and glory ; through JESUS CHRIST our Lord. *Amen.*

Another.

Almighty GOD, grant that in all my dealings with [*here mention him*], I may remember the many opportunities for good and for evil which our close companionship offers. Give us strength to resist all temptations to idleness and sin, to keep ourselves pure in our bodies, and faithful in our lives, that so our companionship may be ever more and more agreeable to Thy Holy Will, and an example to others of which we may never be ashamed; through JESUS CHRIST our Lord. *Amen.*

For Messmates.

Grant, Almighty GOD, to my messmates, the spirit of unity and true godliness. Strengthen and increase the faithful, visit and relieve the sick, turn and soften the wicked, rouse the careless, recover the fallen, restore the penitent. Make us all to be of one heart and mind, bearing each other's burdens, and making allowance for each other's sins. Whatever differences of rank, age, or opinion there may be amongst us, let them not prevent us from setting an example to all men of decency and order; through JESUS CHRIST our Lord. *Amen.*

For the Sick.

O LORD, look down from heaven, behold, visit, and relieve Thy servants in this ship who are sick. Look upon them with the eyes of Thy mercy, give them comfort and sure confidence in Thee, defend them from the danger of the Enemy, and keep them in perpetual peace and safety ; through JESUS CHRIST our Lord. *Amen.*

For a Messmate, or Shipmate, who is very Sick.

O LORD, I beseech Thee to refresh the soul of Thy servant [*here mention him*] who lies grievously sick. Thy will be done with regard to his life on earth ; but give him time and grace, merciful Lord, to receive healing of all spiritual sickness, to repent of all his sins, and to look constantly and faithfully to Thee for pardon and peace ; through JESUS CHRIST our Lord. *Amen.*

For the Patients in the Royal Naval Hospital at Yarmouth.

O Heavenly FATHER, sustain and

comfort Thy servants who have lost the powers of reason and self-control. Suffer not the Evil One to vex them. Impute not unto them the unseemliness of word or action into which they fall. Look upon them graciously, as redeemed by the Blood of Thy dear Son ; and grant that they, finding Him their only wisdom, may be delivered from the darkness of the world, and attain to the glory of Thy Presence ; through the same JESUS CHRIST our Lord. *Amen.*

After leading Some One into Sin.

O GOD, the giver of pardon, I call on Thee on behalf of [*here mention names*], whom I have turned from Thy commandments and led into sin. Require not *his* blood at my hands, but forgive *him* and me all our sins ; give me grace to make what amends I can for my fault, that, sinning no more, we may together escape Thy condemnation ; through JESUS CHRIST our Lord. *Amen.*

Upon the Birthday of a Friend.

Almighty and Everlasting GOD, the

Maker of all creation, mercifully hear my prayers, and grant many and happy years to Thy servant [*here mention by name*], whom Thou didst bring into this life to-day, that he may spend all his life so as to please Thee ; through JESUS CHRIST our Lord. *Amen.*

For Unity in the Church.

O Blessed JESU, who saidst unto Thine Apostle, " Peace I leave with you, My peace I give unto you," regard not my sins but the faith of Thy Church, and grant her that peace and unity which is agreeable to Thy Holy Will, who livest and reignest with the FATHER and the HOLY SPIRIT, one GOD, now and ever. *Amen.*

For the Parish at Home.

O GOD, bless all those in the [*village or*] parish where I was brought up, from whom I am now divided by the sea. Bless the clergy, the teachers, and the Sunday-school. Bless those especially who remember me in their prayers. Grant that we may meet again on earth, if it be Thy will.

But if not here, grant that we may meet in that heavenly country where there shall be no more parting and no more sea; through JESUS CHRIST our Lord. *Amen.*

For Foreign Missions.

Almighty GOD, who by Thy SON JESUS CHRIST, didst give commandment to Thy Apostles that they should go into all the world and preach the gospel to every creature; look with compassion upon the heathen that have not known Thee, and on the multitudes that are scattered abroad as sheep having no shepherd. Give wisdom, courage, and love to all who labour amongst them in Thy name, and grant us grace so to walk that they may have us for an example of a sober, good, and Christ-like life; through JESUS CHRIST our Lord. *Amen.*

For a Private Enemy.

Good LORD, deliver me from the sin of malice and all uncharitableness, and give me grace always to behave towards [*here mention him*] as one Christian should towards another. Shield me from all temptations to provoke him, and give me a heart to embrace every opportunity to be reconciled to him, that he and I may both have our sins forgiven; through the merits of JESUS CHRIST our Lord. *Amen.*

For Shipmates.

Almighty GOD, by whose providence we are gathered together and preserved in this ship, give us grace to acknowledge the daily blessings which we receive at Thy hands. Grant to us the spirit of devotion to Thee and of loyalty to our Queen and country. Fill our hearts with such love towards Thee and towards each other that, whether on deck or in the mess, aloft or below, on board or ashore, we may ever set before us the object of our honourable profession, which is to serve, and (if it please Thee) to die for Thee and our country; through JESUS CHRIST our Lord. *Amen.*

SHORT PRAYERS TO BE USED WHEN WE ARE BUSY ON THE FOLLOWING OCCASIONS.

On Seeing Any One Fall into Sin.

LORD, lay not our sins to his charge.

Or,

Have mercy on us, LORD, for we are weak.

Or,

Teach him, O GOD, that the wages of sin is death.

On Hearing Blasphemy and Bad Talk.

O LORD, open Thou our lips, that our mouth may shew forth Thy praise.

Or,

LORD, open his eyes that he may see the wondrous things of Thy law.

On Hearing Any One Tell a Lie.

From lying lips and from a deceitful tongue, good LORD, deliver us.

Or,

LORD, speak Thou the truth to his heart, that he may confess it with his mouth.

On Seeing Any One Fall Overboard or from Aloft or Struck Down by a Sudden Blow.

JESU mercy !

Or,

LORD JESUS, receive his spirit !

Or,

In the hour of death call him.

On a Death.

Almighty GOD, we thank Thee for Thy servant [*here mention his name*], whom Thou hast been pleased to call to Thyself, and whose soul, as we trust, Thou hast brought into sure consolation and rest ; grant to us, we beseech Thee, the spirit of preparation, to meet Thee when Thou callest us, that at the Day of Judgment, we with him and all thy servants departed this life in Thy faith and fear may be partakers of Thy heavenly kingdom ; through JESUS CHRIST our Lord. *Amen.*

10

VI.

The Sailor's Life Ashore.

ON SHORT LEAVE.

WHEN the liberty men have fallen
in on the Quarter-deck we know that
the devil is unusually active. This is
specially his time of temptation. A
man who is not strong for GOD as he
walks over the gangway is not likely
to be strong for GOD when he steps on
shore. The Seaman is tempted to bad
company, to make sinful engagements
before he goes on leave ; in fact, as
soon as the word is passed for the
liberty men to clean, and even before
then. Let the Seaman remember that
the struggle for GOD has to be begun
afresh at this moment, when parties
are being arranged and chums are
making their plans for the expected
leave. It will need all his watchfulness,
all his faith in GOD, to make the time
on shore a blessing and not a curse.

It is very unwise to go on shore without having some definite plan for
spending the time. If the Seaman has
no idea how he is going to employ
his time during the leave, he stands
in danger of falling into temptation
the moment he lands. This is almost
as bad as making up his mind before-
hand to spend his leave badly ; for
Satan reaps his largest harvest in the
field of idle souls. Let him never go
ashore on leave, therefore, without
using the prayer at page 29, or, if he
be hurried, making one for himself as
he cleans ; and in the spirit of this
prayer let him make his own arrangements, either with his chum, or some
companion whom he can trust, so that
want of company may not be his
excuse for joining the first party of
messmates or topmates he meets.
There is one very common practice
which he should avoid at all risks,
that of going into a publichouse to
drink the moment he gets ashore.
It is scarcely necessary to give a
reason for this. The practice is full
of danger, and it is not to quench thirst

but to promote (as they think) good fellowship that Seamen begin to drink —no matter what hour of the day it is —as soon as they set foot ashore.

The Seaman should look for his lodging early, if he intends sleeping ashore, and not put this off till the night-time when he will be tempted more strongly than ever to put it off altogether. If he has no friends in the port, and has reason to doubt the respectability of the various houses of public entertainment which are within his reach, he should ask for one of the Sailors' Homes, or Temperance Halls, which are so frequently to be found in most seaport towns. If he be at either of the English Home Ports he will have no difficulty in doing this, and by a very little trouble to himself he will be saved much temptation, and consequently much sin. But if he is unable to get a respectable lodging, he had much better come off to his ship and go ashore again early next morning. It may be a little disappointing, especially if he has reckoned on having a good spell of the shore. But he will be amply rewarded the next morning as with body refreshed and clear head he makes for the shore again. Should he be ashore on Sunday, let nothing prevent him from going to Church, and spending his day as quietly and help-fully as he would spend it on board. For the Sunday is the Lord's day to the Sailor as to the landsman, and to the Sailor on shore just as much as to the Sailor on board ship.

Many things have stood in the way of Seamen when they have wanted to go to church ashore, want of know-ledge as to where the nearest church is, the hours of Divine Service ; and, again, the feeling of shyness which every one has on entering a strange public place, to which must be added the idea that the Sailor is not welcomed at church by the other worshippers. But let him find out from the manager of the house, or even by looking on the notice-boards of the churches he passes, what are the hours of Divine Service, and let him then go boldly in whether people welcome him or not. It is his church as much as theirs, and no one has a better claim to worship in it than he.   A little patience and a reverent behaviour will soon read any who might have seemed unkind at first a lesson which perhaps they will remember long and thank GOD for.

This book is not intended to suggest ways in which a Seaman ought to spend his time when ashore, it is sufficient if it helps him to serve GOD ashore so that he may have lost no ground in the battle with sin when he returns on board.   He goes on shore sometimes for business, and sometimes for pleasure.   In truth, it is always a pleasure for those whose life is chiefly spent in the confinement of a ship to enjoy the freedom of the town and country.   And as recreation is as necessary for the Seaman as it is for other men, no check should be placed upon either the amount or the kind of recreation ; let him only remember that recreation is not dissipation, nor is liberty another word for license.   The Christian Seaman knows that he can " enjoy life," whether on shore or on board, all the better for his religion, which he tries to take with him wherever he goes and whatever he does—into his meals and his walks, into his laughter and his prayers, into his reading his newspaper and his reading of GOD's Holy Word.

One sentence more on this head. The Seaman must not be selfish in his pleasures, and though he cannot be too careful in avoiding bad company of all kinds, yet he should before going ashore, and whilst on shore, see if there is any one of his shipmates, and especially any one of his messmates, to whom he can do a good turn. How many a man has been kept from vice and misery, and led too to something better even than this, through the kind action of a topmate, who has induced him to spend his leave with him, and who without preaching or " forcing religion down his throat " has helped him to make his leave really enjoyable, because it was spent soberly and reasonably !

The Christian Seaman must look for such cases, and ask GOD to help him to give up any pleasures on which he has set his heart, if he may act towards them as a Good Samaritan.

Should the Seaman visit any Roman or Greek churches in foreign countries, let him behave with the same reverence with which he would behave in his own church. There will be things which he may be inclined to consider superstitious, especially the pictures and representations of JESUS CHRIST hanging on the Cross. But let him remember that the worshippers are baptized Christians, and that therefore any sign of love or reverence they may shew to the Saviour is to be treated with respect if not with sympathy—certainly not with mockery or contempt. We ought never to enter a church without saying a prayer for the worshippers and for ourselves, that GOD would lead us all "into all truth," and bring us together in the bonds of His love.

Here are two Prayers which may be useful in connection with this subject.

O LORD, we beseech Thee, let Thy continual pity cleanse and defend Thy

Church ; that it may be so guided and governed by Thy good Spirit, that all who profess and call themselves Christians may be led into the way of truth, and hold the faith in unity of spirit, in the bond of peace, and in righteousness of life ; through JESUS CHRIST, who liveth and reigneth with Thee and the HOLY GHOST, now and ever. *Amen.*

Another.

O GOD, righteous and merciful, who wast pleased to deliver up Thine only begotten SON to be mocked, scourged, and crucified, for us sinners ; grant unto us, at the sight of Him hanging upon the Cross, healthful sorrow of heart, that as by our sinning we have slain the Author of our life, so by our repentance we may draw life from His death ; through the same JESUS CHRIST our Lord. *Amen.*

ON LONG LEAVE.

If the Seaman is blessed with a home to which he is welcomed on his return to England, let nothing hinder him from spending his leave in it. The time spent there will be a true refreshment to him. The old faces of relations and friends, the old scenes, the old associations (if they are good ones) will do more than anything else towards driving away the effects of the " salt water." It will be something for his friends to be thankful for and proud of, if they see him taking his proper place—whether as son, or husband, or father, in the old home, and setting an example for good to all whom he meets ; if he is to be found in his seat at church regularly, and shewing by his behaviour that he is not there for pastime ; above all, if he kneels at the Lord's Table and receives the Blessed Sacrament of Christ's Body and Blood, thereby drawing more tightly together the bonds of family or friendship, which may seem to have been loosened by his long absence from home. He will be tempted to go with a multitude to do evil, especially by those who love his money rather than himself. He will be tempted to regard himself a hero on account of the wonderful things ye has seen or done. Let him not hield to either temptation. Let these temptations to idleness and pride be met by a resolve to be quiet and to do his own business, and let him rather strive to shew all men that he is in every way the better for his service in the Navy.

VII.

The Sailor's Helps to a Godly Life.

I.

WHENEVER the ship touches at a port where there is a garrison of English Soldiers, the Christian Seaman should lose no opportunity of making friends amongst them. There is much kindness shewn by the British Soldier to his comrades in the sister service, and many a Seaman has acquaintances and relatives in the different regiments. The privileges of using their canteens, recreation rooms, cricket grounds, &c., are always eagerly embraced by the Seamen. Where there is therefore so much interchange of friendly courtesy between the two services, how very needful it is for this unity and brotherly love to be extended to the highest matters. The Seaman will find in the Soldier a man exposed to many of the temptations which beset himself, and when he is fighting against these temptations, he will find in the Soldier a true companion in arms ; for as the dangers are common, so too are the weapons by which they are best overcome.   The Soldier will often be able to assist the Seaman in this godly work ; and the Seaman, too, will have many experiences which will be of advantage to the Soldier.   And if there is nothing else, there will always be that sympathy which exists between those who are fighting the LORD'S battles shoulder to shoulder.   There is, as a rule, too much shyness in such matters between the two services—too much of a disposition to work in separate ways, to the great waste of strength, and a great loss of love.   In ships where no Chaplain is borne, the Seaman will have no difficulty in getting a soldier-comrade to introduce him to the Military Chaplain, and to the Scripture Reader who is working under him. From these he will receive every sympathy and assistance.   He will be welcomed at the Bible classes, and, above all, at the Holy Communion.

II.

There are Societies, both in the Army and Navy, which aim at bringing Seamen and Soldiers closer together in the bonds of Christian charity, and in their common work for the great Captain of our salvation.   Ask your Chaplain to tell you about them.

A Seaman's Rule of Life on Shore.

I. Never go ashore without resolving to spend your time well. When the word is passed, make up your mind so far as you can what you will do and where you will go, so as not to be taken unawares when you step ashore.

II. Never be seen in places or in company which GOD, through the voice of your conscience, forbids. Think if they are such as your mother, or sister, or wife, or child would approve.

III. Avoid as much as possible all singularity of behaviour, and in your dealings with others act with perfect honesty, gentleness, and purity.

IV. Be moderate in eating and drinking, remembering that when the restraints of discipline are removed, the temptations to gluttony, drunkenness, and impurity are sure to be stronger.

V. In your amusements seek to be strengthened rather than to be excited. In walking, sitting down, or at places of entertainment, remember that the eye of GOD is upon you, not to make you sad, but really happy.

VI. If you see a shipmate or messmate in trouble or in sin, do not be too much occupied in your own pleasure to go to his assistance. If you can do nothing else, you can say a prayer.

VII. Never turn in at night nor out in the morning without saying your prayers. Do not pass a Church, especially on a Sunday, without entering and mingling with the worshippers. If the Holy Communion is not celebrated on board your ship, prepare to receive it at some Church ashore on the first opportunity.

UNWIN BROTHERS,
PRINTERS,
CHILWORTH AND LONDON.

PUBLICATIONS

OF THE

𝕾𝖔𝖈𝖎𝖊𝖙𝖞 𝖋𝖔𝖗 𝕻𝖗𝖔𝖒𝖔𝖙𝖎𝖓𝖌 𝕮𝖍𝖗𝖎𝖘𝖙𝖎𝖆𝖓 𝕶𝖓𝖔𝖜𝖑𝖊𝖉𝖌𝖊.

---

	s.	d
ALONE WITH GOD; OR, HELPS TO THOUGHT AND PRAYER. For the use of the Sick; based on short passages of Scripture. By the Rev. F. BOURDILLON, M.A., Author of "Lesser Lights." 12mo. ....*Cloth boards*	1	6
A MODE OF CATECHIZING. By the Rev. TEMPLE HILLYARD, Rector of Oakford, Devon, Canon of Chester Cathedral. 18mo. ....*Cloth boards*	1	0
APOSTLES' CREED (THE). Aid to its Reception; Duties under it. Being a plain Exposition of the Creed, with some Practical Observations. Eight Lectures. By the Rev. C. J. D'OYLY. *Cloth boards*	1	0
BIBLE PLACES; OR, THE TOPOGRAPHY OF THE HOLY LAND. By the Rev. Canon TRISTRAM, Author of "Land of Israel," &c. A new and revised edition, with Map. Crown 8vo......................*Cloth boards*	4	0
CHRISTIAN MISSIONS BEFORE THE REFORMATION. By the Rev. F. F. WALROND, M.A. With four full-page Illustrations on toned paper. Post 8vo. *Cloth boards*	2	6

[1-1-79.]   [Royal 32mo.]

TURNING POINTS OF GENERAL CHURCH HISTORY.
By the Rev. E. L. CUTTS, B.A., Author of
"Pastoral Counsels," &c. Crown 8vo.
Cloth boards

UNDER HIS BANNER. Papers on Missionary Work
of Modern Times. By the Rev. W. H. Tucker.
With Map. Crown 8vo. New Edition. *Cloth boards*

VENTURES OF FAITH; OR, DEEDS OF CHRISTIAN
HEROES. By the Rev. J. J. HALCOMBE
Cloth boards

WILSON (BP.) ON THE LORD'S SUPPER.
Royal 18mo. Fine Edition, *with rubrics and lines
in red*, cloth boards ....
32mo., limp cloth ....
  Cloth boards, red edges ....
  Levant, gilt edges....................................
  Blue calf, gilt....................................
  Morocco ....

WILSON (BP.) SACRA PRIVATA.
Large type ....
———— coloured sheep....................................
Royal 18mo. Fine Edition, with *red lines*, &c.,
cloth boards ....
  Levant, gilt edges....................................
  Calf, limp or boards....................................
  Morocco, limp or boards....................
32mo., cloth boards, red edges ....
  Levant, gilt edges....................................
  Morocco ....

Depositories :

77, GREAT QUEEN STREET, LINCOLN'S-INN FIELDS,

4, ROYAL EXCHANGE, E.C.;

48, PICCADILLY, W.; LONDON.

Printed in the USA
CPSIA information can be obtained
at www.ICGtesting.com
LVHW050034280924
792338LV00002B/552